Make Money at Art Shows and Craft Fairs

By

A. B. Petrow

Published by Craftmasters™ Books
Sebastopol, California

DISCLAIMER

This publication and associated software are designed to provide accurate and authoritative information with regard to the subject matter covered. It is sold with the understanding that the Publisher is not engaged in rendering legal, accounting, or other professional advice. If legal advice or other expert assistance is required, the services of a competent professional person should be sought.

Every effort has been made to make this book as complete and as accurate as possible, but no warranty or fitness is implied. Neither the author nor Craftmasters Books, nor anyone else who has been involved in the creation, production, or delivery of this product shall be liable for any direct, incidental or consequential damages, such as, but not limited to, loss of anticipated profits or benefits, resulting from its use or from any breach of any warranty. Some states do not allow the exclusion or limitation of direct, incidental or consequential damages so the above limitation may not apply to you.

ISBN-13: 978-0-9655193-2-8
ISBN-10: 0-9655193-2-5

Table of Contents

Introduction

Over the years at craft fairs and art shows, many people have approached me with questions about how to get started selling their own creative artistic creations. Frequently asked questions include: How do you find out about where and when the shows are? How do you get into the shows? Why are some people admitted and others not? Where did you get your canopy and tables? How do I keep track of my taxes?

With this book you have all the information you need to sell what you make, at art shows and craft fairs. With the addresses of over 800 good craft fairs and art shows, you are guaranteed to find people who will appreciate and buy your craft work. If you supply the necessary irresistible handmade products and lots of self-discipline, you will be successful.

I have also included hundreds of tips I learned the hard way, a list of all the craft fair guides, a list of the best promoters with more than one show (if you get in one of their shows you are in all of them), and, if you want to use your computer, some spreadsheets to get organized. All of the forms and spreadsheets described in this book are available for free download on the publishers website at www.craftmasters.com

My intention with this book is to provide you with much more information than I had when I started, so you can start making money in much less time than it took me to learn the ins and outs of this type of business. Good luck, and see you at the shows!

Art Shows and Craft Fairs

"Hey Mable, what the heck are all those tents"
"It's a craft fair, Henry. Lets go see."
"But the game is on TV!"
"You can see the game any time. The craft show is only once a year."
"What the heck is a craft show?"
"Its where people put their nice craftwork on tables so you can look at it."
"Oh, you mean like a flea Market!"
"No, these people make what they sell."
"Can they make a living doing that?"
"Not if we don't go, Henry."
"Dang."

Types of fairs

Basically there are three types of shows:

- The family show
- The craft fair
- The art show

The family show may have carnival-type entertainment, chamber of commerce booths, a craft area, and music. At the craft fair there may be some music, but the emphasis is on art and crafts. The art show usually has only fine art and some fine crafts, with few other attractions (and distractions) for the customer. Many events overlap in other areas as well. For example an art show may have a music group as a lure, or a family show may have a small fine art exhibit. Shows may also specialize in traditional crafts like dried flower arranging and tole painting, or contemporary fine crafts such as handmade gold and silver jewelry, pottery, fiber, and wood turning.

For your first show, you should pick a small local show. You probably won't make much money but you have to start somewhere, to learn what you need in the way of display equipment, comfort, product, etc. This is called "paying your dues." You can even start with a flea market. There are always a few people shopping at a flea market that will recognize quality when they see it, and will give you some valuable feedback about your product, price, and display. Plus you can get rid of a few things cluttering up your garage. Flea marketing of your craft is usually only good for one or two trials, though. For one thing, the people who come each weekend to a flea market tend to be the same people over and over, and after two weeks your sales will drop dramatically.

First, you need a product

You have a product if:
1. It is something you like to make.
2. It is both useful and artistic.
3. It sells for at least five times more than the cost of the materials in it.
4. You can make a lot of them at a time.

(If you want to spend six months making a chair, fine, you might have a work of art, but you don't have a product.) You need a product that people want. If it has a function they will want it even more.

Some Ideas for Crafts

This book was written assuming that you already have a craft that you are fairly proficient at producing. If you don't have any idea what you would like to make and make money at, here is a list of products that have been popular at craft fairs. You might have to take some courses at your local college, get some books about the craft, or find a teacher or craftsperson to teach you and help you get some experience.

MEDIA CATEGORIES

These are taken from two craft fair applications.

Ceramics - Original clay and porcelain work other than jewelry. If multiple pieces of the same design are displayed, the artist must sign each piece. No machine-made or mass-produced work is permitted. 2. Art objects either functional or decorative of earthenware

Digital - Images made with the assistance of computers. Computer graphics are often made with software called drawing, painting, illustrating and photographic programs or applications. Traditional photographs taken with digital media should apply in the photography category.

Drawing/Pastels - Drawings are works on paper using pencil, crayon, ink, charcoal, pastels and a variety of other marking media. 2. Works created using dry media including chalk, charcoal, pastels, pencil, wax crayons, etc., or from a fluid medium of inks and washes applied by pen or brush.

Fiber-Wearable - Includes clothing, or leather goods, such as belts or purses, that can be worn. No factory-produced items, regardless of additional modification or enhancement by the artist, may be exhibited. 2. All work crafted from fibers that is wearable. No machine-tooled, machine-screened patterns or miscellaneous forms of mass production are permitted.

Fiber-Non-Wearable - All work crafted from fibers that is not wearable. No machine-tooled, machine-screened patterns or miscellaneous forms of mass production are permitted. All factory-produced wearable items, regardless of additional modification or enhancement by the artists, are not accepted in this category. 2. Includes non-wearable artwork from fibers such as basketry, embroidery, weaving, tapestry, and papermaking.

Graphics or Printmaking - Printed works for which the artists hand manipulated the plates, stones or screens and which have been properly signed and numbered as a limited edition may be entered in this category. Printmakers are required to disclose both their creative and printmaking processes. Digital art applicants may apply in this category. 2. Printmaking is a transfer process of producing original art, usually in multiples. It involves creating a drawing or other composition on a surface other than paper, for transfer to paper through the use of a press or through impressions made by hand.

Jewelry - Ornaments, such as bracelets, necklaces, or rings, made of precious metals set with gems, semi-precious gems, ceramic, glass or any other product. Jewelry must always enter in this category and not in glass, ceramic, etc. that may be the type of material used – jewelry is always jewelry. 2. All jewelry, whether produced from metal, glass, clay, fiber, paper, plastic or other materials. No commercial casts, molds or production studio work is allowed.

Glass - Glass works that are functional or decorative by design and are kilnformed or have been crafted by glass blowing, molding or casting. Works may be etched or engraved. No forms of mass production are permitted. 2. The expression of art made from blowing, fusing or otherwise fashioning glass.

Metal - Creating artwork through the forging, twisting and fabricating of various metals.

Mixed Media 2-D - Includes any combination of a variety of materials to create an original two dimensional work of art. 2. Two and three-dimensional works that incorporate more than one type of physical material in their production. This includes nonsculpture work as determined by the artist.

Mixed Media 3-D - Includes any combination of a variety of materials to create an original three dimensional work of art.

Painting: Oil/Acrylic - Creation of a still life, portrait, landscape, abstract or other image on a flat surface, such as canvas, with oil and/or acrylic paint or sticks. 2. Works created in oils and/or acrylics.

Painting: Watercolor - Creation of a still life, portrait, landscape, abstract or other image on a flat surface with watercolors.

Photography - Process of capturing images of objects by the action of light, then printing the images, by chemical or digital means, onto a flat surface. 2. Photographic prints made from artist's original negative that have been processed either by the artist or under his/her direct supervision. Photographers are required to disclose both their creative and printing processes.

Sculpture - Shaping figures or a design in the round or in relief, by chiseling marble, modeling clay, casting metal or other materials. Three-dimensional original work done in any medium.

Wood - Art objects, either functional or decorative, that may be hand-tooled or machine worked in wood, turned or carved.

Craft show myths

If you are thinking along any of the following lines as you contemplate a successful craft fair business, forget it. You may be able to pull it off, but you will not be a success.

1. I will buy some imports and sell them as my own.
2. I will just show up at a fair without first applying, and they will let me in.
3. I will find a successful craftsperson and copy them.
4. I will make something that the stores have and sell it cheaper.
5. I will put my crafts on the Internet and won't have to do shows at all.
6. Being a successful craftsperson is easier that working at a job.
7. I will make only what I like. If the public likes it fine, if not, fine.
8. I can read and relax at a craft show, because I work all week.
9. I don't need to take Visa or MC, just cash.
10. I can sell crafts and avoid taxes.

All of the above are wrong!

How to find out where the fairs are

Visit a craft show advertised in your area and ask the artists who the promoter is. Also ask which shows they recommend, and which ones to avoid. Find out if the show is better for high-end crafts, or traditional arts and crafts, and how long the show has been going on. Subscribe to a craft fair guide.

You can also search Google on the internet with some general keywords like "craft fairs (your state)." You will be surprised how many listings pop up.

Tips for finding a good show

Use www.festivalnet.com.

The membership fee is about $50 a year. Search the site by state and month, and you will see all the shows in that state for that month. One way to tell if a show has potential is by the booth fee. If it is under $100, it is probably too small of a show to make much money. One rule of thumb is that you should make 10x the show fee for it to be a good show.

Get the Art Fair SourceBook

After you have been doing shows for a while, and you want to travel to bigger shows in other states, this book is very helpful in telling you what to expect at a show. It gives you tons of information about each of the top 300 shows in the country. A subscription for one year is around $200.00. www.artfairsourcebook.com 800-358-2045

Regional craft fair guides

Every area in the United States has one or more craft fair guides, magazines that report on fairs for several states in that region. A few guides specialize in fairs only in a single state, and some others try to cover all of the best fairs in the entire country.

Some guides, such as the Art Fair Source Book and Sunshine Artists, try to rate the shows, based on reports of income and user reviews. Others just list all the shows equally, with contact information and number of attendees, etc. You have to try to figure out on your own if the show is worth doing, using booth fees and attendance as a guide. Of course, even if the show is rated, your experience selling your particular craft may be very different.

Craft Fair Guides

NAME OF DIRECTORY	STREET	CITY	ST	ZIP	CONTACT	PHONE	AREA COVERED
Crafter's Blue Book	P. O. Box 513	Kechi	KS	67067	DJ Wallace	888-206-6311	CO, KS, MS, OK, IL, MI, NE, SD, IA, MN, ND, and WI
Festival Network Online	P. O. Box 18839	Asheville	NC	28814	Kirt Irmiter	800-200-3737	United States and Canada
The Crafts Fair Guide	P. O. Box 39429	Downey	CA	90239		562-869-5882	California, Arizona, Nevada, and Oregon
The Crafts Report	300 Water Street	Wilming-ton	DE	19801	Bernadette Finnerty	302-656-2209	United States
Art Fair Source Book	2003 N. E. 11th Ave.	Portland	OR	97212	Greg Lawler	800-358-2045	United States
Your Show Guide	P. O. Box 11795	Casa Grande	AZ	85230	Mary Davidson	520-836-8427	Arizona, Colorado, and Nevada
Festivals Directory	P. O. Box 7515	Bonney Lk.	WA	98391	Carol Farer	253-863-6617	WA, OR, ID, MT
Sunshine Artist Magazine	3210 Dade Ave.	Orlando	FL	32804		407-228-9862	United States
The Network Marketing Guide	P. O. Box 1248	Palatine	IL	60078	Teresa or Nancy	847-604-3965	IL, MI, rest of the nation.
Extravaganza Craft News	160 Green Tree Dr.	Belgrade	MT	59714	Shasta McLaughlin	406-388-9883	MT, ID, WY, North and South Dakota
Art and Craft Show Yellow Pages	P. O. Box B	Red Hook	NY	12571	Betty Chypre	888-424-1326	Ct, MA, NJ, NY, PA, VT.
Wisconsin Art and Craft Fairs Directory	101 E. Wilson Street	Madison	WI	53702		608-266-0190	Wisconsin
Craftmaster News	P. O. Box 39429	Downey	CA	90239		562-869-5882	CA and other western states

How to choose a good fair

With so many fairs to choose from, it is a challenge to pick a good fair. My philosophy is to try almost any fair (if I have some indication that it might be good), and see what happens. If it is not good, I don't have to ever do it again. Sometimes a little-known fair will surprise you with a lot of sales. To try and minimize the bad fairs, I have a few basic criteria. Number one, I like to know a lot of people will be there. 10,000, 50,000, 120,000, 600,000 people. With enough shoppers I can usually make money at any show. Show me the people! If you have a more expensive product, then you might focus more on areas where the customers have more disposable income. This could be a smaller indoor art show that is sponsored by an art guild and has an excellent reputation, or a show in a very wealthy area. Again, experience counts. You have to be willing to try any well-reputed show at least once. That is the only way to know if your product and price is a match for that customer base.

To calculate the potential of a show, multiply the attendance number by $10 (half of the people will spend $20 and half will spend nothing) and divide it by the number of artists. 50,000 people times $10 equals $500,000 divided by 250 artists equals an average of $2,000 per artist.

The application process

The first step is to get the fair's application. This doesn't cost you anything. Write to every fair that you might want to do, and ask for an application. I recommend sending a simple typed letter with your name and contact information. This enables the show producer to get your address right. The letter need only say "Please send me an application and any information about your upcoming shows, and put me on your mailing list. Thank you." Print fifty copies of the same generic letter, sign them, and mail them to the shows that you might be interested in. You don't have to impress the promoter in this letter. They will gladly send an application to anyone. Sometimes, if you waited until the last minute, the fair can fax you an application or you can get it online.

When you receive the application, the next step is to make a deadline list with the name of the fair, deadline date, and fair date on a sheet of paper, posted in a place where you will see it. There is a form for this in the spreadsheet section of this book. You then file the fair application in a folder with the name of the month on the folder that the fair is going to happen. When your deadline list shows that the fair application deadline is coming up, you go to the fair's folder, take out the application, fill it out, and mail it in.

Read and complete the application

Read the entire application when you get it. If you don't, you will often miss little details, such as "send in a resume," or "don't send anything in but the application," or even "include a slide of your workshop." It might be hard to get a good slide of your workshop at the last minute. Fill out the application completely and neatly. Many promoters have told me that they get a lot of incomplete and/or unreadable applications.

Slides

How important are slides? **Extremely important!** Simply put, the better the show, the better your slides must be to get in. Although there are still a few good shows that are filled simply by the promoter looking at photos on her kitchen table, all of the best shows are juried.

A jury consists of 2 to 12 artists, promoters, art teachers, and local experts who sit in a darkened room while all of the slides are projected simultaneously on a wall or screen. As the three-to-six slides are shown, each judge gives points for design, creativity, craftsmanship, etc. The process often takes less than 20 seconds for each artist, with the promoter reading the descriptions of each slide supplied by the artist if necessary. Often the acceptance of the artist is based solely on these points.

What is the jury looking for?

The jury is looking for good slides, first and foremost. This is the big hurdle. And of course, the jurors are looking for creativity and originality. Good slides won't necessarily get you into good shows, but bad slides are likely to keep you out.

The first thing the jury notices is the quality of the slide. A poorly lit or badly composed slide might not look so bad under home viewing conditions, but at a jurying the slide is instantly compared with the expertly photographed slides already shown that day. So the first impression is important. A juror will be less impressed with unprofessional slides, and they will give fewer points. No matter how nice the craftwork is, you are wasting your time and money with poor quality slides.

All slides should be consistent. Each slide should show only one craft item, shown close-up, filling the screen, and well exposed. There is a strong desire in beginning craftspeople to show many items, five or six in each slide. They want to show the jury the range and variety of their design. But the juror will see only clutter. You have to pick your best pieces.

The same is true for the background. All of your slides should have the same background. Beginners love to put rocks, flowers, bricks, and other stuff in the picture. They also like to photograph on a fancy cloth or carpet background. They hope the attractiveness of the background will make their craft look more attractive. The opposite will happen. The juror will be confused, not impressed.

Photography

You can make your own photographs with either a 35mm camera or digital camera. If you don't already have film camera experience, I would suggest that you go the digital route. Get a digital camera and have slides made from your images if and when you need them. You can use your digital files for online applications, Zapplications, web galleries like etsy.com, and your cards and brochures.

Your digital camera doesn't have to be fancy. You can use nearly any digital camera made in the past three years with 3.2 mega pixels or more. It might be more useful if it has manual settings so you can control your depth of field. Most digital cameras have scene settings that will provide you all you need for a good image. For example, Kodak has a flower setting that takes excellent photos. The Olympus SP550 has a setting for auctions that works great. Make sure it has macro capabilities. Macro is indicated by a flower symbol.

The biggest advantage of a digital camera is that you can practice to perfection without it costing you a dime. You will need to learn a little about lighting. And you will need to learn about digital manipulation with a photo editing program.

If you need slides, you can correct your digital photos in Photoshop or Elements, and email the files to www.slides.com. They make slides from your digital files for around $2.50 each and FedEx them back to you. Slides are 3:2 ratio. The best resolution for making slides from digital is 4096 x 2730. If you need prints, use photo paper in your printer.

If you don't want to spend the time and money to get good photo results on your own, hire a commercial photographer that specializes in craft or small product (table-top) photography.

Hap Sakwa
403 Taft St., Sebastopol, CA 95472 (707) 823-5787
Craftspeople all over the country send him products to be photographed.
www.hapsakwa.com

Jerry Anthony
Excellent craft photography. 3952 Shattuck Avenue, Columbus, Ohio 43220
(614) 451-5207 info@jerryanthonyphoto.com

Azad
Azad Photography
Specializes in jewelry 660 Laramie Blvd. Boulder CO 80304 (888) 258 0657
www.azadphoto.com

George Post
George Post Photography.
5835 Bouquet Avenue. Richmond CA 94805 (510) 237-0197
gpp@gpostphoto.com www.gpostphoto.com.

Bob Barrett
4 Julia Avenue
New Paltz, NY 12561 (845) 430-8599
www.bobbarrettphoto.com

If you decide to take your own photographs, here are some tips.

Always use the optical zoom, somewhere in the middle of the zoom range. The optics are better in the middle. Move the camera, not the zoom. Never use the digital zoom.

Override the camera's light meter if possible. The built-in light meter in the camera will overexpose dark items, and underexpose light items. Always use the highest resolution setting in the camera.

Always use a tripod. Greater depth of field requires a slower shutter speed, and the longer shutter opening time increases the chance of camera shake. Use either a cable release or the camera timer so you won't shake the camera and get a fuzzy picture.

Use a neutral background. Don't use plaids, weavings, etc. Uncluttered is the key. Indoors use white, gray, or black (never use red), outdoors use white roll paper or a white sheet. Use a canopy in bright sun to provide even light. It will act as a giant soft box.

Use gradient paper for the background. You can find gradient paper at Superior Specialties, 800-666-2545 **www.superspec.com** I like the #9, black to white, and the #37, blue to white.

Use a commercial lens cleaning cloth on your camera lens. Anything else can and will scratch the coating on the lens.

Write down settings for every shot you take. Save your notes for future reference. To learn with your digital camera, take a photo at every setting in your camera, take notes, then look at all the images in Photoshop or Elements. Go with the setting that makes the best image.

Use a light tent. EZcube Light Tents provides even lighting. They are available on eBay for $45 to $90, depending on the size. You can get a smaller one for jewelry and small items, or use a cloud dome from Rio Grande.

Unless heat would harm your product, use photoflood bulbs and reflectors. Use two or three 500 watt bulbs for indoor shots with a big light cube and 250 watt bulbs with a smaller (18") light cube. Position one on each side and one at the top. Never use the built-in flash on your camera.

You should turn off all fluorescents and as many other room lights as possible, so you control the lighting. If you use film, if there is a fluorescent light on anywhere in the room, it will add an unwelcome green tint to your photo if you use film.

Depth of field is the area of the image that is in focus, from front to back. If your camera has an "A" setting (aperture priority setting), set your f-stop at f16 or f22 and the camera will set the shutter speed. Everything will be in focus. If you want to focus on one special detail of your work, or blur the background, use f4 for less depth of field.

Look at your images as a group. They should have a consistency of vision. Check out the color relationships. Are they interesting? Do they grab your attention? Look for a theme. The jury will.

Booth shots

When a show has two qualified applicants in the same media, and the jurors can't decide, they will go with the best looking booth.

Use a wide-angle setting for booth photos. Stand on a stool if necessary. Shoot your booth shot from a slight angle. Remove all clutter. Make your product stand out. Compare your booth shot to your product photos. They should be the same quality. No people should be in the booth photo. The top of the booth should not show in the photo. The jurors don't care what canopy you use.

Overexpose outdoor booth shots. If you don't, the booth will look dark because the automatic meter in the camera will under-expose for the sky. Better yet, keep the sky and canopy out of the photo altogether. A cloudy day will provide even light, which is best. Use a canopy wall on the ground in front of the booth (out of sight of the camera, of course) to reflect more light into the booth.

Use flash on indoor booth shots. Try to get light into the corners of the booth. You can use your photofloods, if you keep them out of the photo.

Zapplication

Many of the larger shows are using the zapplication process for online screening. Membership is free. You don't need any special software (except for photo editing), but you do need an email address and a credit card when you apply to shows. When you want to apply to a show, you simply go online, type in a brief description about your craft, select the photos you want to apply with, and pay the application fee with your credit card. Their web site, www.zapplication.org, is very helpful with detailed information. Zapplication has about 15,000 artist profiles. One nice feature is that they email you about upcoming shows by email. Another is that you don't pay booth fees until acceptance.

Images for Zapplication must be square, 1920 pixels on each side, and under 1.8 mb in size. You can take your own digital pictures at your highest resolution, crop them square, adjust the levels to change the contrast, and resize them to 72 ppi (pixels per inch) by 1920 pixels x 1920 pixels with Elements or Photoshop. While any 3.2 mega pixel digital camera will work, 6 to 10 mp is better. The photos should be saved to .tif or .psd as you work on them, and when you are finished, saved for the web as baseline .jpg's.

If you use film, you can either have your slides digitized by your local lab or scan them yourself on a home scanner. Make sure they are saved as .tif files. Since your photos have to be square for Zapplication, and 35 mm slides are rectangular, you will have to add black strips on each side of vertical slides or the top and bottom of horizontal slides to make them square. Basically you make the canvas behind the slide square, and black, to provide the stripes. The zapplication.org web site explains how to do this. There are at least 15 professionals listed at the zapplication web site that will convert your slides for you for a fee.

Artists can apply through ZAPP™ by following these steps :

1. Prepare your artwork images formatted to the Image Preparation specifications.

2. Create a profile by entering basic contact information and creating a username and password to ZAPP™.

3. Upload up to 40 digital images of your artwork to your image portfolio.

4. Select your choice of participating shows to apply to.

5. Choose the required number of images to apply to a specific show from your image portfolio.

6. Pay the application fee online with a credit card or mail a check.

7. Submit the application online.

8. Receive e-mail notifications when your applications have been received, and jury results.

9. View your application status at any time on the "My ZAPPlications" page and choose to accept or decline show invitations on the site.

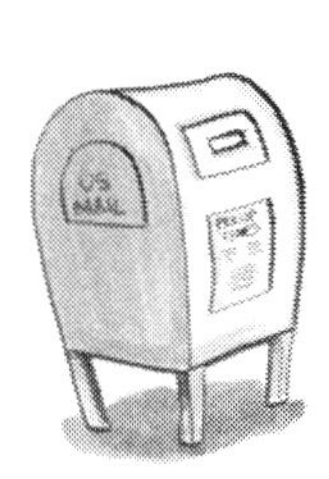

Get the application in on time

A detail often overlooked when reading the application is the "must be received by' or "must be postmarked by" date. Don't wait till the deadline date to discover that the show wants the application in their office by that date, instead of merely postmarked with that date. At any rate, plan to get the application in the post office at least a week early if you can. That way you will have enough time (if you didn't read the application when it arrived) to get the required workshop slide, or price list, or photocopy of ID, etc

Tips for getting into the show

Apply to the show early. Some shows jury slides in the order they arrived at the office, or by postmark. Jurors might look at over 5,000 slides in a few days and they become bleary eyed after a while. You want them to be impressed with your slides while they are still alert.

Make your descriptions precise. If the show asks for a 25-word description for each image, don't write more or less. Your description will probably be read to the jury. If it is too long, it won't be read in full, and if it is short, you are missing an opportunity to tell the jurors what they can't see in your slides, such as process, texture, materials, use, etc. Zapplication allows a 100 character description to be read to the jury.

Use slides of your most colorful and interesting work, to grab the jurors attention. They are comparing your work to all the other work submitted. They usually have only 5 to 20 seconds to look at your slides. Sometimes there are several rounds of judging, with each round eliminating a group of artists. Jurors pay attention to detail, artistic mastery of materials, structure, concept, whimsy, originality, and how everything works together.

Planning your booth

One way to get up to speed about what kind of booth to use is to visit a craft show. Look around at the types of booths and the booth designs. What display looks simple, with the craft dominating, and what looks crowded. Which booths are attractive? Which artists seem busiest? The customer, when faced with a hundred booths and not enough time to examine all of them, will go to the most attractive and interesting looking booth.

Don't be afraid to ask other artists where they got certain items or how they use them. Also ask them how they hold down their canopies, where they got their display showcase, etc. Don't bother them when they are busy, and limit your questions to only a couple at each booth. Most artists and craftspeople love to share information about their booths (when they have time, of course).

Indoor booths

If you are doing indoor shows only, then a booth frame with drapes or other wall covering is required.

A workable combination indoor/outdoor booth is a white E-Z UP with the top off indoors (and the center top pole removed). It should have a Velcro-attaching top, as the bolt-on top is a real pain to remove, and you do not want a top in indoor shows. A lot of people will have much more elaborate displays, and scoff at this suggestion. However, I think the E-Z UP is good because:

1. It is very sturdy. It won't fall into your neighbor's ceramic or glass booth. (Note that we are talking indoors here.)
2. It has a lot of places from which to hang lights and drapes.
3. You can hang banners across the front to cover the lights and the frame. You can also make cloth socks to cover the legs.
4. It goes up in a flash, leaving you more time to work on the other parts of your display.
5. You don't have to keep track of a lot of corner pieces and rolling poles.
6. You don't have to rent pipe and drape, which adds $70 to $140 to your show fees.
7. You can use it for your outdoor shows as well.

Lighting

All indoor shows provide electricity. At some shows you have to pay extra, at others you don't. Some shows require a union electrician and $65.00 just to plug in and turn on your lights!

Most artists use track lighting with halogen bulbs. Halogen lamps cost about $8 each. They give more light and show colors accurately. They also use less electricity then regular light bulbs. Halogen lamps are available in spot or flood configurations. Most booths have a 500-watt maximum. Ten 50-watt halogens will light a booth much better than six 75-watt incandescent bulbs. Gooseneck lamps look unprofessional.

Office Depot has 24" light bars that have three bulb holders. You can also get track in 4-foot lengths and light units for about $16 each. Attach the track with string ties to your booth poles. Make sure your booth lights don't shine in the customer's eyes.

Always use a three-prong extension cord, and grounded 5-plug power strips. Never use two-prong extension cords. If the electrician requires a grounded (three-prong) wire on your lights, and you have only a two-prong plug, you will have to add a ground wire. Run a wire from the metal part of your light along the original wire and attach all three wires to a three prong plug. Have someone who is knowledgeable about electricity to help you with this.

Outdoor booths

Economy--The best display for the least buck is again the E-Z UP canopy. It sets up in a hurry. You can usually find a quality canopy with durable walls and a carrying bag for under $500. If you do 25 shows a year for four years, your cost is $5 per show. If you get one with white-coated metal and a Velcro attached top, you can also use it indoors.

As for the top, make sure it is not a color canopy. A purple canopy will make all of your products look purple, a blue one will give them a blue tinge, etc. Don't use a canopy that does not have the legs straight up and down. The blue-top canopies with legs that point out look really out of place in a professional craft show.

International E-Z UP, Inc.

1601 Iowa Avenue, Riverside, CA 92507 (800) 45-SHADE
They are the distributors for the E-Z UP canopies. Call them for the number of your local dealers. One California dealer is Made in the Shade, P. O. Box 231, Cool, CA 95614 (916) 888-7970. Another is Hawaiian Sun, Inc., Box 5447, Louisville, KY 40205 (502) 458-5066. The strongest heavy duty E-Z UP is called the Eclipse, 70 lbs, best for outdoor shows. The Express is the lighter version (51 lbs), with the removable top, best for flying or indoor shows.

If they are in season at Costco or Sam's Club, the Caravan (or EZ-Up Lite) is cheaper, around $200, and works for all but the windiest shows. They are lightweight and waterproof. They come with four sides, an awning, a bag with wheels, removable top, and a white coating on the metal parts.

Professional--The Light Dome, from Creative Energies, is very heavy duty. The cost is around $800.00 with 4 walls and carrying cases. The frame weighs about 35 lbs, and the walls about 8 lbs each. The top is 14 lbs, so the whole canopy weighs just over 75 lbs. You can use it anywhere, indoors or out, it goes up relatively fast, it is lightweight, and it looks good. It is also the most sturdy. I have been in shows with hurricane-force winds that had every tent flapping in every direction with the exception of one well-anchored light dome, which didn't even move. You can also use a Light Dome indoors. The large round cross-poles hold drapes and lights.

Creative Energies, Inc.

1607 N. Magnolia Ave., Ocala, FL 34475 (800) 351-8889

Craft Huts are used by artists who sell in hurricane areas. They have steel legs and will not leak. Always use the top cross brace on a Craft Hut. If you don't, the arches can blow in toward the middle, and the top will fill with water during rainstorms and collapse the entire tent. They are available from Flourish.

Flourish Co.

RT. 1, Brashears Jct., Combs, AR 72721 www.flourish.com (800) 296-0049
Arch top canopy, Promaster indoor booth frames (with both tabs and screws at the corners for better stability), and flame-resistant drapes. They also have metal mesh walls for hanging art.

City streets

The best anchor for city streets is weights. Thirty five to fifty pounds per corner will usually be enough. Some craftspeople nail the legs of the canopy with concrete nails directly into the asphalt, or use screws with washers and an electric screwdriver. Many shows expressly prohibit this (today's nail hole is tomorrow's pothole). The promoters may not mention it to you, but you might not get back into the show. I recommend weighting two or more corners with 70 pounds each, then have an extra 70 lb. weight in the middle of the booth, with a rope tied to the top (for E-Z UPs). Concrete blocks weigh 34 lbs. Any wind that can move this much weight can move almost any amount of weight, so if a storm is expected, and you don't have tall panels, lower the canopy to half-height overnight (another handy feature of the E-Z UPs and Light Domes).

Always have a weight handy when you set up. You should tie your booth to either it or to an immoveable object in case of a sudden gust of wind. Attach weights to top of tent as well as legs. When weights are used only on the legs, the tent can still twist in the wind.

You can use 8-gallon plastic water containers for weights. 8 gallons of water weighs about 65 lbs. Get the ones with handles (sporting goods, camping stores, or RV stores). Fill them with water at a gas station or food booth when you get to the show and dump them at the end of the show. Carrying empty cans will save you gas, since less weight in your vehicle increases your gas mileage.

You can also make your own weights with PVC. Fill a 6" diameter PVC pipe, 36" long, with concrete, using an end cap and a 12" eyebolt with a washer on the other end. It can be tied to the legs of the canopy (no tape on canopy legs) or fastened to the upper frame with a rope. Some artists like as much as 100 lbs. on each corner of their display. Don't use 3" or 4" pipe—you'll be wasting your time with light weights. You can also fill a 5-gallon bucket with concrete and use an eyebolt in the same way.

Grassy parks

Tents in a grassy park are the easiest to tie down. Use dog stakes. A dog stake is a corkscrew-like device available at pet supply stores that is screwed into the ground. Put two stakes on the two corners that face the wind, and another in the middle of the tent. The middle one is screwed in before the show, but it is only used when the wind comes up. A rope is quickly tied to it and looped over the top of the canopy frame. This beats standing there holding your canopy as the wind blows it around. You can still use additional weights, if you have them.

In a large tent

Some outdoor shows have huge big-top circus-type tents that everyone sets up their booths under. The Asparagus Festival in Stockton, California, the Columbus Arts Festival in Ohio, and the Jazz Festival in New Orleans have big tents. Some tents have room for your E-Z UP inside of the tent. Be sure to remove your top for more light, and remove your peak pole so you don't put a dent in their tent. Occasionally a tent show will not allow E-Z UPs or a full size 10 x 10 booth. You will still need something to hold your walls up and to keep them from flapping into your neighbor's booth. You might have to make or buy a conduit frame to make a booth nine and one-half feet on each side by seven feet high. Flourish also sells these. You will need a wall for the front at night, unless they drop the tent walls.

Weather

You are going to have rain and wind at outdoor shows. The best protection from rain is a canopy with walls. Everything should be stored in Rubbermaids. If the corners of the top of your E-Z UP start to collect water, a large clamp on the top of the inside frame will usually prevent puddling. Wind will either blow your canopy away or blow things out from under it. The best tie-down is to something already there, a rail, a tree, park bench. If you are next to a really heavy booth, ask them if you can tie your canopy legs to theirs.

The worst scenario is when you have both wind and rain. This is one reason why a lot of craftspeople only do indoor shows. But they are missing a lot of opportunities to make money. All a windy and rainy show means is that you need a little more weather protection. The sun will eventually come out and you will make money.

On hot days, bring an ice chest, ice, and lots of water. You can add an awning on the side of your canopy that gets the most direct sun, to shade your products and yourself. Portable AC or DC fans will help keep you and your customers cool.

A weather radio can be purchased at Radio Shack for less than $50. Ask a local at the show which county the show is in, as weather reports are given by county.

Banners, booth signs, and photos

A banner is a great help to people trying to find your booth. It also helps them decide whether to come over to the booth in the first place, when there are so many booths to choose from. The banner should say something about the contents of the booth, not simply the name of the artist. Unless the artist is relatively famous, the banner should say "Handmade Wood Bowls" or "Wood Bowls by Dana Andrews," not just "Dana Andrews."

You might need two banners. They help people find you if they came to the show looking just for you. One cloth, about one foot high by five feet long that hangs across the top of your canopy on a rope. You can take it down at night, when you don't want anyone to know what is in your booth. The other is vinyl, 2 1/2 feet high and 9 feet long, with your product and signature on it. It is used primarily for outdoor fairs when a potential customer may be 50 feet or more away from the front of the booth. Have it made at Kinko's, with grommets on the corners. Attach it to 10' conduit poles with bungees, and attach the poles to your canopy legs with clamps.

An artist's statement is an 8 1/2" by 11" sheet of paper displayed in a clear acrylic stand on your table or hanging in your booth on the wall. It should have a photo of you working in your shop and your name and address at the top. The rest of the page should tell the customer a little about you, how your craft is made, what materials you use, and something about your motivation and purpose. Many fairs are requiring it in your booth. Some customers love to read it completely while waiting. Others might even want a copy, if you feel like handing them out. Send a copy of this statement with your show applications, unless the show specifically states that you should only send slides and nothing else. A few shows are requiring an artist's statement with your application.

Every booth should have a sign about 12" by 24" with the name of the artist and where the artist is from, hanging in the back of the booth. Some shows provide them, but I like to bring our own in case they don't. A sign that indicates the town and state you are from is a good conversation starter. Seeing your name in large print is useful to the customer writing a check.

Always have a photo of your workshop somewhere in the booth. It can be little or big. When asked, "Do you make these yourself?" point to the photo and say, "Yes. Here is a picture of my shop and the tools I use." This is also a great conversation starter. People are very curious as to how and where you make your product.

Many artists with small products have large photos of their products hanging up in their booth. These are helpful for people who can't get quite close enough to see because of the crowd. You can get a slide or print blown up to a 20" x 24" poster at Kinko's for under $40. Have them laminated on both sides. They will hang easier in your booth and won't be as damaged by water. For indoor shows, mount them on foam core from an art supply store. Use grommets and strong thin wire to hang up your photos to keep them from ripping or falling down.

More display ideas

Use drop down bamboo rollups for walls. 8-foot rollups attached to your EZ-up frame with curtain hooks will make your booth seem cozier. They allow air circulation on a hot day, while providing some privacy from the booth next to you. You never know who your neighbor is going to be. The only drawback is that 8 feet is too long for most cars without a luggage rack. 2 four-foot rollups per wall can be used instead.

Use dark curtains indoors. The background should not be noticeable. If not black, burgundy and neutral colors are best. Use white walls outdoors. White will reflect light into your booth and brighten up your crafts in the shade of your canopy.

You can hang a curtain over a back corner of your booth, and use the space for a changing room or storage.

Fireproof your tablecloths. Many indoor shows require this. I have never seen the fire department actually test the cloths. You should have the spray handy in case they do. Fire retardant paints and sprays are available from Flamort. They will provide a certificate for the fire marshal. **www.flamort.com** (510) 357-9494.

DMG Products

(215) 393-8701 Fire Retardant -- fabric spray, wood spray, specialty cloths

Dealer's Supply

P. O. Box 717, Matawan, NJ 07747 (800) 524-0576
(Free 20-page catalog) Fire retardant, showcases, fitted table covers, booth signs, alarms http://www.dlrsupply.com/products.htm

Display items at various heights. This increases the visual appeal of your booth. Small items in your booth should be closer to eye level. Makes your crafts easy to reach. Pedestals are available from Armstrong Products in Oklahoma-800-278-4279 www.armstrongproducts.com.

Have signs in your booth. An artist's statement, credit card acceptance, discount policy, name of business, etc., communicate your business in writing to your customers. They also give customers something to read while you are talking to other customers.

After you set up, step back and see if your booth looks cluttered. If so, simplify it. Hide boxes and carts. Some promoters require this, and it benefits you as well.

You should use a tall chair. Every time you get up from a low chair you put stress on your back. You should be able to just slide forward off of it. The seat should be at least 30" high, so you are eye-level with the customer. I like Gold Medal canvas director chairs and the aluminum chair from www.dickblick.com.

Take prints of your past creations and put them in a portfolio or scrapbook along with pictures of your studio. Customers can browse this while waiting.

Make your table taller, so your customers don't have to bend over to see your products. The closer to customer eye level the better. You can use PVC tubing to make leg extensions.

O'Brien Manufacturing

2081 Knowles Road, Medford, OR, 97501 (541) 773-2410

Oak and glass cases of many shapes and sizes for wall, table, and countertop. Excellent quality, and fast delivery. We have been using their 12" deep by 24" wide by 18" high oak cases for years.

Daniels Display Co., Inc.

1267 Mission Street, San Francisco, CA 94103 (415) 861-4400
Power track lighting and tempered glass case systems. These are the glass display systems with the chrome metal connectors that are repositioned with a wide blade screwdriver. You can make your own shelves from clear plastic. Useful for transporting when space is at a premium.

Packaging

Provide gift boxes whenever possible. If your product is useful as a gift, display a few boxes and offer them to every customer, especially around Christmas, Father's Day, Mother's Day, etc. If the customer is looking for a gift and sees the product already in a nice gift box, you have just provided a solution. The gift box may stimulate the customer to think of your product as a gift and then think about who to give it to.

Rio Grande

7500 Bluewater Rd. N. W. Albuquerque, NM 87121. (800) 545-6566. They have quality packaging and display for small products.

Every product you sell should be put in an attractive bag. The customer appreciates it. You should have two sizes of bags, a small one that holds one or two products, and a big one that holds more. Offer to hold the customer's purchase while they check out the rest of the show.

Uline

2105 South Lakeside Dr.Waukegan IL 60085 (800) 958-5463 Every size of box, bag, shipping label imaginable. Fast shipping. www.uline.com (free catalog).

Provide a hang tag with information about how the product was made, what it is made of, how to care for it, who made it, and how to get in touch with them. This tag should also fit neatly in the gift box.

Taking VISA and MasterCard

You should try to get set up to take charge cards as soon as possible. At some shows your income will be 80 or 90 percent from VISA or MasterCard sales. There are two ways to take credit cards:

1. Run the card through a portable imprinter at the show, and then key or call in the sales when you get home.
2. Run the card through a portable wireless terminal at the show, which clears the card through a cellular connection.

You will need a business account with a bank, and permission from them to take cards in your business. The bank is going to give you the money from the cards before it is actually collected by them, so you must have good credit. If your bank won't let you take credit cards, there are several choices:
1. Get another bank. If you have $2,000 cash to open a business account with, make it clear to the new bank that your opening the account is contingent on your being able to process credit cards. They will take you seriously if they want your business. You tell them that you will be taking the cards at trade shows or at shows in your home. They will probably visit your home to see if you really have a business. They may also want to see a business license or resale permit.
2. Go directly to a credit card company. Novus Services, a company associated with Discover Card, will set you up directly with them, and they send the money from the card charges directly to your bank. Their phone number is 1-800-347-2000. They will let you take MasterCard and VISA in addition to Discover. They give you a portable imprinter and sell you a Trans 330 terminal for about $300. You imprint a charge slip from the card at the show in the imprinter and give the customer a copy. Later at your motel or home, you key the numbers from the card into the Trans 330, which is hooked up to a phone, and they give you an authorization number clearing the card. They charge you about 2.4 % of the sale amount. They are anxious to get more business, and more likely to sign you up than a bank. American Express is a separate company, and their charges must be processed separately. They too are actively looking for new businesses. They have a separate imprinter for their shorter charge slips.

Portable credit card terminals

Credit card processing fees are cheaper (1.8%) when cards are run through a portable credit card terminal and cleared immediately, than when run through an imprinter and called in by phone (2.8%). The reduction in fees and reduction in losses from bad cards will pay for the terminal in a year or two. The time you save by not calling in the cards after the show, and the peace of mind from having the card cleared at the show, make the cost of the terminal worthwhile.

One company I recommend is Total Merchants Services. Their number is 888-848-6825. They, as most merchant service companies, provide the Lipman Nurit 8000 GPRS. It is completely portable, and uses either rechargeable batteries or can be hooked up to AC Power. The 8000 can be connected to a phone line in your office, or works with wireless when you are at a show. The cost of the terminal is normally around $750.

Some merchant providers will loan you the terminal, but charge higher fees. For more information, go to http://www.totalmerchantservices.com. Be sure to buy an extra battery for $70, which could come in very handy at a show.

The customer's charge card is processed immediately by sliding the card through the terminal, and a charge slip is handed to them to sign. A copy of the slip is printed for a receipt for the customer. The terminal clears the card in about seven seconds. At the end of the day, the credit card company processes the batch of charges and deposits the money from VISA and MasterCard into your bank account. At the end of the month you receive a statement from the company detailing your sales by card type. Most companies charge an additional capture fee for American Express and Discover cards for clearing their cards. They may take a few days longer to appear in your account. You have to set up the accounts with American Express and Discover separately, and then your terminal will take all of the cards.

Tips for taking credit cards

Put up "Credit Cards Accepted" signs. Some people walking the show are looking for this notice. They might have run out of cash at another booth, or simply didn't bring any. By the way, never charge extra for charge card usage. It is illegal to charge a customer extra for using a credit card. However it is not illegal to give a discount for cash.

Check the customer's credit card for their signature. If it isn't signed, have them sign it before you use it. If you are suspicious, ask to see their driver's license, and compare the signatures. Some customers prefer not to sign their credit cards. You can't force them to do so, but remind them that a thief could sign their name for them, and then the "false signatures" would match.

Bring a manual credit card machine (knuckle buster) and charge slips for backup. If your electric credit card machine fails, runs out of paper, etc, you will still be able to take credit cards. When you use a manual credit card machine, try to get a phone number and address. It is illegal to require a credit card user's phone number, but you can ask them to put it in your address book for your mailing list. Then you will be able to call them if the slip is unreadable or lost (or if they left something in your booth). If you run out of charge slips when on the road, go to a local bank for more charge slips.

When using a manual credit card machine, always check the charge slip for clarity. Check to see if the number and expiration date is clear. Some cards have worn numbers, or the numbers have been tampered with (flattened). Sometimes the machine might not imprint the whole number (which you must check when you fill out the slip). When you get home to call the charges in, if you don't have the whole number, you won't get paid.

Keep all credit card sales receipts. Store them in a separate envelope, with the name and dates of the show written on it. If the charge is disputed, the signed original will be easier to locate.

Selling tips

Explain the benefits of your product to the customer. People buy for personal benefit. Theirs. Not to do you a favor. Not because you are good looking or well dressed. They benefit from your product, or they pass it by. They might visualize how comfortable it will feel in their hands the next day when they pick it up. Or they will visualize being perceived as individualistic because they have or give a one-of-a-kind object, or as an art lover who has actually met the artist who made the item, or as a meticulous person who buys well-crafted items. This is where the large photo of your item being used is helpful; it shows the customer how he or she will benefit. It is simply a matter of the price of the item matching the benefits of the item to the customer.

Don't read a book in your booth. It is too absorbing. A magazine might be okay, as the articles are shorter and don't require as much attention. A magazine about your craft, Metalsmith or Fine Woodworking for example, is beneficial to both you and the customer. You learn some new techniques while waiting for a sale. The customer will think you are up-to-date on your craft. If a magazine is prominently placed in your display, the customer might even infer that you are featured in the magazine. No harm there. Someday you will be. If you already are featured in a magazine, by all means, display it.

Avoid excessive sales pressure. Some customers might walk into a booth where the artist is preoccupied, but be reluctant to walk into a booth where the artist is staring at them and appears too eager to jump up and start trying to sell them something. Always say a couple of words to the customer, such as “Feel free to look closely,” or “Try using it.” After you get the product in their hands, give them time to examine the work, give them the details they ask for, and maybe a suggestion that the item would make a good gift, and that you have gift boxes. Then leave them alone again. People really appreciate feeling un-pressured in a shopping environment. Just imagine how you want to be treated when you shop. You want to be helped when you need it, but you don't want a salesperson hovering around you all the time. Do the same for your customers.

Whenever a customer asks how the show has been for you, tell them you are doing well, even if it is the worst show you have ever done. Even the bad shows have some benefits, such as learning frugality or humility, so you won't necessarily be lying. Never complain to the customers. There is nothing they can do about it.

When a customer asks you which one you recommend, always suggest a mid-range item, and they will immediately trust you. Never recommend the higher priced item. They will be suspicious and you will be scrambling to explain why it is better. Of course, your attitude indicates that all of your products are of excellent quality and priced at exactly the right price.

Give them a reason to buy today. Offer them a small discount (under 5%) if they buy now. Say, “It is always good to have some gifts around in case you need them for an unexpected occasion.” To encourage an immediate sale, don't give out business cards (except for the "care and contact information" card you give the customer after the sale).

Assume everyone has a credit card. That means they have the money to buy your item, unless all of their cards are maxed out. Be sure that you tell them you take charge cards and they can see your VISA card signs or terminal.

Listen to your customers. They notice if you are not. If you are already dealing with a customer, and a second customer interrupts, ask the first customer if you can talk to the second one. Deal with the question politely, and then get back with your first customer.

Educate your customer. Art sales involve 50% education and 50% sales technique. Most people visiting your booth have no idea how you do what you do. Tell them why your work is worth the price and how hard it was to make.

Be prepared to talk your head off. Don't let a few know-it-alls discourage you. A raw material in the hand is worth a thousand words—show a block of laminated wood, bag of clay, carving wax, etc.

If you have an environmental angle to your product, describe it. Conservation of resources is very important to some people. Tell them how you use materials economically.

Tell a story about your product. They want to know what inspired you to make it and how hard it is to make. Have photos of your shop to show them. Tell how successful the product has been for you.

Maintain eye contact with your customer. If you are looking all around the show, they will too.

Never judge a customer by their appearance. Every artist has a story about the customer who dressed and acted like a hobo, but bought a very expensive item.

Remind people if it is the last day of the show. There are customers at every show who think the show goes on forever.

Use key words to make sales. Some comfortable key words are "warm, soft, clean, powerful, bigger, better, and yes." Yes, I have a gift box. Yes, I take charge cards. Yes, I have a trash bag.

Offer a hesitant customer a guarantee. Offer a full refund or replacement if customer is dissatisfied.

If people ask for your card, hand them a guest book to write their address and email in. You can contact them later with a postcard or catalog.

On the road

Many artists prefer to travel to shows in a van. A van is not much longer than a car when it comes to parking and getting in and out of the show set-up area. But if you ever need to nap or camp overnight, you may have that option with a van, and not with a car. Also, when you are driving a van, you have better visibility, and everyone on the road can see you better. And, of course, you can haul a lot more stuff. The drawback is are that you use more gasoline. Astro vans and Chevy vans seem to be more reliable. You can design a booth to fit in your car, but it is better to get a vehicle that will carry a booth designed for maximum sales of your products.

I don't recommend sleeping in rest stops on the freeway at night. There is no security at a rest stop. If you are traveling and all rooms are booked up, park or nap in a truck stop. Almost every truck stop in the U. S welcomes RV's (and vans). The bigger ones have 24-hour restaurants and free showers with a fill-up. More and more truckers are husband and wife teams, and truck stops cater to them. The restaurants at some of them (Pilot) have all-you-can-eat buffets for $8.00, and phones at every booth. Most have a security guard. The bathrooms are cleaner and safer. The main drawback is truck noise. You either have to park as far from trucks as you can, or get earplugs.. You can hook your computer up at a booth and check your email. Just act like you own a big rig. ;-)

Things to bring in your car or van:

Fire extinguisher. You can also keep it in your booth during the show.

Phone charger that works from the cigarette lighter..

A road atlas from a truck stop.

An AAA or AARP card to save money on towing and rooms.

Jumper cables. Get 12 gauge, not 14 or 16, and the longest ones they have.

Tire gauge. Low tire pressure can affect your steering.

Tire jack and a lug wrench. Learn to change your own tire.

Gloves and coveralls to wear to change the tire.

A working flashlight.

Oil, transmission fluid, and power steering fluid.

A spare alternator belt. (NAPA Auto Parts) will tell you which one.

Extra keys in a magnetic case under the car.

A first aid kit with Tylenol, aspirin, tweezers, antiseptic and Band-Aids.

Car alarm and steering wheel lock (Le Club).

Vehicle security on the road

Get an alarm for your vehicle. It should have an engine kill switch, remote, window stickers and a flashing red light visible to thieves when it is armed. Alarms cost less than $250 installed. I am always surprised that more artists don't have one.

If you have a trailer, get a lock for both the hitch and the bar. Paint a number on top of your trailer to help the police find it if it is stolen.

Join a tow service--Allstate, AAA, or Good Sam. The Good Sam Club Emergency Road Service is about $100 a year. This includes towing, gas, flat fixing, and lost keys. Their number is (800) 234-3450. The number for AAA is (800) 922-8228, Sears Allstate Motor Club (866) 209-0394.

Flying to Craft Fairs

Flying to a craft fair has many advantages. You can do a show anywhere in the country, whenever you want. Otherwise, if you drive to shows in another part of the country, you have to line up several in a row to make the trip worthwhile. Once you figure out how to fly to a show, you just pick the best ones around the country, fly there, and fly back. Plus, you get more time in the shop.

Some crafts are easier to fly with than others. The lighter and smaller your product, the easier it is. But don't let a heavier product stop you from the big shows. The trick for big crafts is to ship your product by air cargo, rent a van when you get to the show, pick up the products with the van, and there you are, van and products, on the other side of the country, on the same day. The last time I checked, you could ship by Delta air cargo for 60 cents a pound. You can get help loading and unloading from Labor Ready, 4 hours for $60 (800-245-2267).

If you have small crafts like jewelry, carry them in a rolling carry-on bag with a handle and a small daypack. They both have to fit through the x-ray machine, and be small enough to stuff in the overheads. Never leave anything valuable in your checked luggage

Yes, you can fly with your canopy. It must have a cover on it. Bring your products with you in your carry-on luggage, and check the canopy with the rest of your luggage at the baggage counter. You will have to pay $80 for each additional bag over two. Delta and Southwest seem to have the most liberal luggage polices.

Get a fiberglass trunk (Contico) for selling supplies, gift boxes, and clothes.

The next trick is getting everything into a cab, your car rental, or the airport shuttle. Pick up some concrete blocks from Home Depot to hold down your canopy when you get there, and you are all set.

Book your roundtrip flights with www.travelocity.com. Priceline is not as good for flights because you can't choose your exact time of travel.

Book rooms with www.priceline.com, usually cheaper than Travelocity, and guaranteed better quality. Offer a ridiculously low price; you just might get it. Start with four stars and $60.00. Then three stars for $50, then two for $40 or less. Only ask for one area with your first offer. You can't raise your price without changing something, so if you don't get your price the first time you can add another area or reduce your stars and then slightly lower your bid. Don't be afraid of two star rooms. Two star motels like Extended Stay America are usually newly constructed, have kitchenettes with cooking utensils, and sometimes go for a bid of $32.00. You won't get kitchenettes with a three star bid. Start a month before the show, because if all of your bids don't work, you have to wait three days to bid again.

Be sure to print out your online airline and hotel reservations. Take them with you. Sometimes the hotel or motel computer doesn't get the information in time.

You can get a portable lightweight table from postergarden.com, or make your own table that fits in a suitcase with light-weight tubing and thin plywood.

Abstracta Structures, Inc.

347 5th Avenue, New York, NY 10016 (212) 532-3710
www.abstracta.com Tubular steel structural systems for displays, exhibits, store fixtures, and furniture.

More Craft Fair Tips

Before the show

Make a checklist of show necessities. Always check your list just before you leave home.

A sample list of show necessities:
Gift boxes
Hang tags
Bags
VISA machine, thermal paper, and charger
VISA signage
Calculator
Sample of work in progress
Banner
Stakes
Booth sign
Statement of purpose (artist's statement)
Price stickers
Duct tape
Rope
Pocket knife
Clamps
Other handy stuff:
Phone charger
Camera, card, and batteries
Umbrella/raincoat
Mosquito repellant
String ties
Super glue
Floor mats
Hand cleanser
Windex
Garbage bags (for end of the show clean-up)
Paper towels
Gloves (for tire changing, etc.)

Call ahead if you are going to be late. Otherwise, the promoter might give your space away.

Setting up for the show

Use a hand truck with large tires for easy loading. Big wheels roll over cracks better. Magline carts are the best hand trucks. They have big wheels, 2 or 4 wheel positions and hold up to 800 lbs. Priority Supply Company, 2127 Lake Lansing, Michigan 48912 (517) 374-8573.

Never put tape on the legs of your E-Z UP. The sticky residue left will prevent you from closing it down after the show.

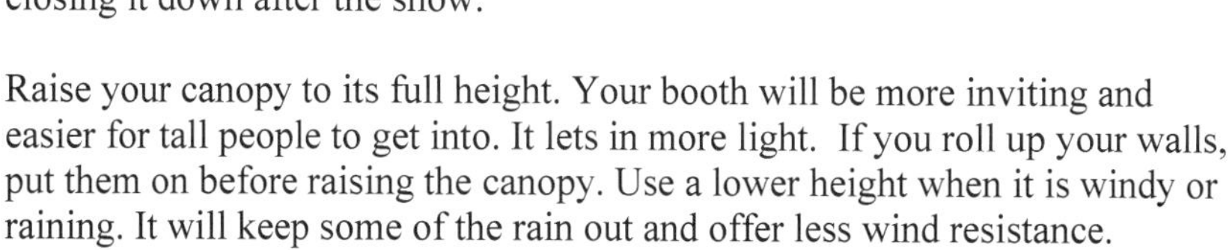

Raise your canopy to its full height. Your booth will be more inviting and easier for tall people to get into. It lets in more light. If you roll up your walls, put them on before raising the canopy. Use a lower height when it is windy or raining. It will keep some of the rain out and offer less wind resistance.

Use a combination stool/tool box for tools. If you dedicate a set of tools for shows, and keep them in a combination stool/toolbox, you will always have the tool you need and the stool also helps you put up walls, curtains, and lights at the show.

Floor coverings make everyone more comfortable. A 4'x 6' oriental rug in darker colors will make your booth look more elegant and make your feet less tired at the end of the day. Tape the front edge.

During the show

Be in your booth early. At outdoor shows, if you spend 60 minutes in your booth before the show is officially open, ready to help customers, and stay open a little longer in the evening, it adds up to four extra hours in a three day show. Or, one extra show for every six shows, at no extra cost to you.

Ask people what they think of your new items. Do they like the color, the price, shape, etc.? Pay close attention to their comments. This type of feedback is one of the great advantages of doing a retail craft fair or art show.

Keep your display out of the aisles. Don't put anything in front of your booth, and don't sit in the aisle, as it restricts the flow of traffic to the booth next to you.

Never criticize other craftspeople. Nothing looks more unprofessional to customers or other craftspeople.

Get a 50% deposit for custom work. Full payment in advance is even better.

Give a small price break for multiple purchases. Customers want to think they can get a better price if they are buying directly from the artist. But you have to be firm. You might be dealing with a "flea market" personality, someone who never ever pays full price. Ten percent is a reasonable amount for three or more items. Don't offer it unless you think it might encourage them to buy. If your first reasonable discount offer is rejected, don't make another. Explain again why your product is better.

Never sell seconds. They will come back to haunt you, especially if your customer gives them to someone else, who doesn't know they are seconds, and brings them back to you to fix. It is better to have the "Everything I sell is perfect." mentality. People don't want flawed items for gifts.

Don't use "Sale" signs at a fair. The public expects that the price asked reflects the artist's time and materials. If items are on sale, you have to explain why. Many promoters forbid sale signs.

Start a mailing list. At shows, collect names and addresses with a guest book. Use either a nice address book or notebook with large spaces for the customer to write big. Copy into a database all addresses from both the guest book and the checks you receive. Someday you will have a huge mailing list. At least once a year, send a postcard to everyone on your list, with information about your shows, web site, or new products.

You can make your own guest book. Print headings horizontally on a sheet of paper for name, address, phone, email, and anything else you want to know, and have Kinko's copy it and make a book for you, or put the copies in a 3-ring binder.

Never charge extra for gift boxes, etc. The customer will think you are cheap and resent the charge. Customers like the word "free."

Always fill out the show survey when available. It is your best chance to get the promoters to improve the show. Don't just write your complaints. Give helpful suggestions on how to improve the show. If they don't know what is wrong, how can they fix it?

Don't rush to pack up after a show ends. After 45 minutes, 75 percent of the other artists will be gone and out of your way. In addition, you might make a few more sales from latecomers. If you rush to get home after a show when you are tired, you are more likely to have an accident.

Avoiding theft

Keep valuables out of reach. Thieves will reach under your table or in from the back of your booth. Put your purse or camera out of sight in a rubbermaid or a large trunk. Attach your purse strap to a table leg, canopy leg, etc. Purse-snatchers at fairs are looking for a purse that is unattached.

Don't use a cash box. Keep your money (at least all paper money) in a pocket or a fanny pack. Keep coins, but not bills, in a simple box for sales tax change. It will make noise if it is stolen.

Separate large bills from small bills. Keep large bills in a separate safe place that is harder to access, a different pocket, etc. This keeps you from accidentally giving someone big bills with their change, or spilling the money on the ground.

You are more vulnerable to theft when packing up. You are separated from your products when going to your vehicle, and again when the products are in the vehicle and you are back at the booth. Ask your neighbor to keep an eye on your booth. Lock your car doors anytime valuables are inside.

Use a locked storage box or trunk. A Contico fiberglass foot-locker (Linens 'n Things or Walmart) can be locked in your booth with a padlock and bike chain attached to your table or something heavy. Put things like your credit card machine and calculator in it for overnight storage. If a drunk or prankster gets in your booth at night, they probably won't try to get into it.

Health

At the first sign of a cold, take lots of vitamin C. 3,000 mgs a day should keep the cold at bay. Also take a multiple vitamin and a baby aspirin every day. Aspirin is also useful in reducing strokes and heart attacks.

Mercury vapor lighting can cause migraines. Those lights can also cause a green tinge in your booth. Use your own halogen lights to improve your lighting. Bring Tylenol.

Do yoga stretches to avoid a bad back.

Drink lots of water during a show. Dehydration will cause headaches and soreness. Water also helps to combat the low humidity of indoor shows.

Aetna Health Insurance

Lower rates for self-employed people. www.aetna.com 866-549-INFO

Promoters of Multiple Fairs and Shows

Send all of the promoters of multiple shows in your area a letter asking for information or an application. Many of them screen (jury) you only once, then if they like you and your products, you can do as many of their shows as you want without being re-screened for each show.

PROMOTER	ADDRESS	CITY	ST	ZIP	PHONE	# OF SHOWS
DeSoto Caverns Park	5181 DeSoto Caverns Pkwy.	Childersburg	AL	35044	800-933-2283	2 outdoor
Elise Blackwell	116 Al-Jo Curve	Selma	AL	36701	334-874-8044	1 indoor, 2 outdoor
Hillbilly Corner Arts, Crafts	22530 Deer Run Rd.	Hindsville	AR	72738	501-789-5726	2 indoor, 2 outdoor
Fourth Avenue Merchants Assoc.	329 East 7th Street	Tucson	AZ	85705	520-624-5004	2 outdoor
Magic Bird Promotions	P. O. Box 1803	Cave Creek	AZ	85327	480-488-2014	1 indoor, 8 outdoor
Mill Ave. Merch. Association	P. O. Box 53046	Phoenix	AZ	85072	480-967-4877	4 outdoor
Mountain Artists Guild	P. O. Box 12920	Prescott	AZ	86304	520-445-2510	2 outdoor
The Events Group	P. O. Box 328	Tempe	AZ	85280	602-968-5353	5 outdoor
Thunderbird Artists	15648 N. Eagles Nest Dr.	Fountain Hills	AZ	85268	480-837-5637	7 outdoor
Beckman's Gift Show	P. O. Box 2337	Los Angeles	CA	90027	323-962-5424	4 indoor

California Artists	P. O. Box 1963	Burlingame	CA	94011	650-348-7699	15 outdoor
Clovis Chamber of Commerce	325 Pollasky Ave	Clovis	CA	93612	559-299-7273	3 indoor
Custom Productions	P. O. Box 800524	Santa Clarita	CA	91350	661-297-0119	1 indoor, 5 outdoor
Eckerstrom Productions	4908 Blank Road	Sebastopol	CA	95631	707-829-5064	10 outdoor
Hartman Studios	P. O. Box 70160	Point Richmond	CA	94807	510-970-3217	4 outdoor
Harvest Festival	601 North McDowell Blvd	Petaluma	CA	94954	707-778-6300	15 indoor
Jan Etre Presents	P. O. Box 9188	Berkeley	CA	94709	510-526-7363	1outdoor, 1 indoor
MLA Productions	1384 Weston Rd.	Scotts Valley	CA	95066	831-438-4751	3 outdoor
Pacific Fine Arts	P. O. Box 280	Pine Grove	CA	95665	209-296-1195	12 outdoor
Piecemaker Country Store	1720 Adams Ave.	Costa Mesa	CA	92626	714-691-3112	4 outdoor
R.G. Canning Attractions	P. O. Box 400	Maywood	CA	90270	310-835-9370	24 outdoor
Ray Leier	3051 Via Maderas	Altadena	CA	91001	626-797-6803	6 outdoor
Sandpiper Prod.	P. O. Box S-3053	Carmel	CA	93921	831-620-1281	2 outdoor
Scenic Art Shows	P. O. Box 485	Chino	CA	91708	909-623-5977	4 outdoor
Show Biz Productions	16520 Harbor Blvd. #D-2	Fountain Valley	CA	92708	714-418-2000	4-6 indoor
Steve Powers and Company	P. O. Box 1610	Pismo Beach	CA	93448	805-481-7100	8 indoor
Village Artisans	P. O. Box 1448	Bakersfield	CA	93302	661-328-1943	2 indoor
West Coast Artists	P. O. Box 4389	Chatsworth	CA	91311	818-709-2907	22 outdoor
West Fest Productions	100 So. Sunrise Way #145	Palm Springs	CA	92262	760-321-2148	20 outdoor
Adams County Historical Society	9601 Henderson Rd.	Brighton	CO	80601	303-659-7103	3 indoor
Chun Capital Hill People's Fair	1490 Lafayette St. #104	Denver	CO	80218	303-830-1651	1 outdoor
Cortez Area C of C	P. O. Box 968	Cortez	CO	81321	970-565-3414	2 outdoor
Denver Merchandise Mart	451 E. 58th Ave. #470	Denver	CO	80216	303-292-6278	2 indoor
Downtown Denver Partnership	511 16th St. #200	Denver	CO	80202	303-295-6330	3 outdoor
J&J Promotions	8490 W. Colfax Ave. Box 33	Lakewood	CO	80215	303-232-7147	3 indoor
Keystone Art Festival	P. O. Box 38	Keystone	CO	80435	970-496-4570	1 outdoor

Howard Allan Events Ltd.	9695 W. Broward Blvd.	Plantation	FL	33324	954-472-3755	40 outdoor
Monticello-Jefferson C of C	290 North Jefferson St.	Monticello	FL	32344	850-997-5552	2 outdoor
The Handmade in America Show	251 Creekside Dr.	St. Augustine	FL	32086	904-797-2600	20-30
United Production	125 5th Ave. N.	Safety Harbor	FL	34695	727-725-1562	4 outdoor
Hilltop Productions	481 Millard Gainey Road	DeFuniak Springs	FL	32435	850-951-2148	20 outdoors
Andersonville Gld.	P. O. Box 6	Andersonville	GA	31711	912-924-2558	2 indoor
Blue Ridge Mountains Arts	P. O. Box 1016	Blue Ridge	GA	30513	706-632-2144	2 outdoor
Contemporary Crafts Market	1142 Auahi St. #A7-2820	Honolulu	HI	96814	808-422-7362	3 indoor (in CA)
Downtown Davenport Assn.	102 So. Harrison St.	Davenport	IA	52801	319-322-6268	4 outdoor
Festivals International	508 4th Ave. No.,	Clearlake	IA	50428	515-357-5177	2 indoor, 4 outdoor
Personalized Wood Products	P. O. Box 193	Amana	IA	52203	319-622-3100	2 outdoor
Buhl Chamber of Commerce	716 Hwy. 30 East	Guhl	ID	83316	208-543-6682	2 outdoor
American Society of Artists	P. O. Box 1326	Palatine	IL	60078	312-751-2500	12 indoor 15 outdoor
Craft Show Promotions Inc.	302 Allen Ave.	West Chicago	IL	60186	630-293-3637	3 indoor, 9 outdoor
Bright Star Promotions	3428 Hill Vale Rd.	Louisville	KY	40241	502-423-STAR	20 indoor
Steinhauer Productions	16471 Hwy 40	Folsom	LA	70437	504-796-5853	15 indoor 2 outdoor
Artisan Promotions.	83 Mt. Vernon St.	Boston	MA	2108	617-742-3973	3 indoor
Americana Arts and Crafts	15 Cypress Street	Hagerstown	MD	21742	301-791-2346	7 outdoor
Buyers Market of American Craft	3000 Chestnut Ave. #300	Baltimore	MD	21211	410-889-2933	2 indoor
Sugerloaf Mountain Works	200 Orchard Ridge Dr., #21	Gaithersburg	MD	20878	301-990-1400	8 indoors
White Oak Plaza Merchants	923 So. 7 Hwy.	Blue Springs	MO	64015	816-118-6620	4 indoors
Forest Grove Community Club	P. O. Box 16	Forest Grove	MT	59411	406-538-8348	2 indoors, 1 outdoor
Lewiston C. of Commerce	P. O. Box 818	Lewistown	MT	59457	538-5436	2 outdooor
Bele Chere Festival	P. O. Box 7148	Ashville	NC	28802	828-259-5800	3 outdoor
High Country Art & Craft Guild	P. O. Box 2854	Asheville	NC	28802	828-254-0072	11 indoor 1 outdoor

Downtown Comm	P. O. Box 962	Fargo	ND	58107	701-241-1570	1 indoor, 1 outdoor
Huffman Productions Inc.	P. O. Box 184	Boys Town	NE	68010	402-331-2889	9 indoor
Kimberly Ann Kreations	RR1 Box 200	Hoskins,	NE	68740	402-565-4583	2 indoor
A.C. A. C.	P. O. Box 650	Montclair	NJ	7042	973-746-0091	6 outdoor
Rose Squared Inc.	12 Galaxy Ct.	Belle Mead	NJ	8502	908-874-5247	8 outdoor
Lovington Chamber of C.	201 S. Main	Lovington	NM	88260	505-396-5311	2 indoor-outdoor
Mill Museum	P. O. Box 287	Cleveland	NM	87115	505-387-2645	2 indoor inoutdoor
The Walker Organization	3340 Wynn Rd. Suite D	Las Vegas	NV	89102	702-364-1174	3 indoor
Williams, Ltd.	4790 Caughlin Pkwy., #507	Reno	NV	89509	775-324-6435	5 indooor 25 outdoor
American Arts & Crafts Alliance	45 Riverside Drive #15H	New York	NY	10025	212-866-2239	3 outdoor, 2 indoor
American Craft Council	21 South Eltings Corner Rd	Highland	NY	12561	800-836-3470	7 indoor
Artrider Productions	P. O. Box 28	Woodstock	NY	12498	914-331-7900	8 indoor, 1 outdoor
Cord Shows, Ltd.	4 Whipporwill Lane	Armonk	NY	10504	914-273-4667	2 indoor, 2 outdoor
Designer Arts	114 Mill Road	Red Hook	NY	12571	800-660-1045	5 indoor
George Little Management	Ten Bank Street	White Plains	NY	10606	914-421-3206	5 indoor
Soho Antiques Fair & Crafts	P. O. Box 337	Garden City	NY	11530	212-682-2000	52 weeks a year
Washington Sq. Outdoor Art	115 East 9th St. #7C	NY	NY	10003	212-982-6255	2 outdoor
Raab Enterprises	P. O. Box 33428	N. Royalton	OH	44133	440-237-3424	30 indoor
Tom Danner Event Mgmt.	P. O. Box 1473	Marion	OH	43302	740-389-5707	2 indoor
Benton County Fairgrounds	110 SW 53rd St.	Corvallis	OR	97333	541-757-1521	6 indoor, 1 outdoor
Brookings Chamber	P. O. Box 940	Brookings	OR	97415	541-469-3181	1 indoor, 1 outdoor
Eugene Sat, Mkt.	76 W. Broadway	Eugene	OR	97401	541-686-8885	14 in/35 out
Jefferson County Fair	P. O. Box 237	Madras	OR	97741	541-475-4460	2 indoors
Oregon Homecrafters	P. O. Box 70333	Eugene	OR	97401	541-343-6856	5 indoors
Rogue Valley	P. O. Box 4041	Medford	OR	97501	888-826-9868	weekly

Sisters Area Chamber of C.	P. O. Box 430	Sisters	OR	97759	541-549-0251	1 indoor, 4 outdoor
Umatilla County Fair	P. O. Box 94	Hermiston	OR	97838	541-567-8115	1 indoor, 1 outdoor
Umpqa Valley Arts Association	P. O. Box 1105	Roseburg	OR	97470	541-672-2532	2 indoor, 2 outdoor
BJ Promotions Belle Shilling	RR#1, Box 1772	Union Dale	PA	18470	570-679-3670	40 indoors
Heritage Markets	P. O. Box 389	Carlisle	PA	17013	717-249-9404	15 indoors
Renaissance Craftables	541 Woodland Dr.	Radnor	PA	19087	610-687-8535	4 indoor, 4 outdoor
Country Fairs	6311 So. Canyon Rd.	Rapid City	SD	57702	605-343-8783	5 indoors, 1 outdoors
Festival in the Park	P. O. Box 648	Spearfish	SD	57783	605-642-2311	1 indoors, 1 outdoors
Esau, Inc.	P. O. Box 50096	Knoxville	TN	37950	865-588-1233	2 indoors
Tennessee Assoc of Craft Artists	P. O. Box 120066	Nashville	TN	37212	615-665-0502	3 outdoors
American Country Shows	P. O. Box 1129	Fredericks-burg	TX	78624	830-997-2774	25 indoors
Art Promotion Counselors	P. O. Box 776	Alamo	TX	78516	956-787-6996	30-40 indoors
Events Mgmt. Group, Inc.	P. O. Box 8845	Virginia Beach	VA	23450	757-486-0220	3 indoor
Craft Producers	P. O. Box 300	Charlotte	VT	5445	802-425-3399	3 indoor, 9 outdoor
Jim Custer Enterprises, Inc.	P. O. Box 14987	Spokane	WA	99206	509-924-0588	4 indoors
Metro Parks, Tacoma	4702 So 19th St.	Tacoma	WA	98405	253-591-5484	3 outdoors
One Reel	P. O. Box 9750	Seattle	WA	98109	206-281-8111	2 outdoors
Showcase Northwest	P. O. Box 2815	Kirkland	WA	98083	800-521-7469	3 indoors
Wisconsin Indian Head Country,Inc.	P. O. Box 628	Chetec	WI	54728	715-924-2970	5 indoors 4 outdoor

General Business and Marketing

Bookkeeping

All you need is a Dome Simplified Monthly Bookkeeping Record. You can get one at a stationery store or by calling (800) 432-4352. It meets all IRS requirements for record keeping. You simply enter monthly expenditures on the left, income on the right, and add up the totals at the end of the year or tax time. There are two extra pages for expenses for each month. Just tear them out and write the name of the month in the space provided on the income side for each month. They don't have Dome Books at Office Depot or Office Max anymore. The Atlas accounting books they sell only have one column for income, and they don't hold up very well.

Accounting programs separate all deductions into categories. You don't need separate account numbers. If the item is deductible, simply write it down in your Dome book. All that is needed for a deduction is a date, item, and amount (and a receipt).

Use basic commercial receipt books. Use a rubber stamp with your company name and address, phone number and email. Gallery buyers are not as impressed with your sales forms and invoices as they are by timely delivery and fast turnover.

If you fill out your phone orders by hand, you won't have to wait for your computer to boot up in time to take the order.

Back up your mailing list. Keep duplicates (including account information) in a place separate from your workplace or office. In case of fire or theft, you won't have to recreate everything.

Taxes

You have to pay taxes if you have a craft business. The IRS considers a business as any activity that makes a profit in 2 out of 5 years. If you don't make any profit with your crafts, it is considered a hobby and you can't deduct your craft-related expenses. You can get more tax information free direct from IRS. Get IRS publication 334 "Tax Guide for Small Business."

All of the interest on a business credit card can be deducted on your Schedule C. Your business credit cards don't have to be in your business name, just earmarked for business use.

A Dome book has a very comprehensive list of everything that is deductible. The bottom line is, if you use it to assist your business, deduct it. The Schedule C tax form also has a list of deductions.

Don't deduct for business use of your home. Since this is the most abused tax deduction, it is a red flag for the IRS, and the deduction (a percentage of the rent for a room in your house) is usually not large enough to be worth it.

Keep track of your bank deposits. In a field audit, the IRS will add up your bank deposits for the year and compare them with your stated gross income.

Check if a "Home Occupation" business license is required. In most cities, even if you don't have employees, you may still need a business license to work out of your home. If you have employees, or the public comes to your studio, you might need to have your studio in a commercial zone.

If you have employees, you need an employee identification number (EIN) from the IRS. 1-800-829-4933. If you don't have employees, you can use your social security number for business purposes whenever an EIN is asked for.

You will definitely need a state sales tax number or ID. Write, call, or go to the state office of taxation in your state. This is where you will send the sales tax you collect in your state.

If you want to do business under a different name than your own, get a fictitious name statement from your county offices. You can usually do this online. In most states you will have to publish the fictitious name in a newspaper.

Copyright

You should try to copyright your work. Copyright costs $20.00 and protects graphic or sculptural works for 70 years after the artist's death. Copyright forms are free and available from Library of Congress, U. S. Copyright Office, 202-707-9100. Their general information number is 202-479-0700. www.lcweb.loc.gov/copyright.

Copyright your catalog with a "Visual Arts" form. All of your designs will be protected for your life plus 70 years. www.loc.gov/copyright.

You can't copyright function but you can protect it. Utility patents are good for 18 years. www.uspto.gov.

If you can't copyright your work, you might be able to get a design patent to protect your work. A design patent is good for 14 years. You can't get a design patent for anything that has been in public view for over a year. www.uspto.gov 202-707-9100

Use a "TM" after your company name. Do this even if you haven't registered the name yet, but intend to.

Always put a copyright notice on your work. It should appear as "Copyright 2007 by Bob Smith." The date refers to the first use of your product. Put it on your printed materials and your products.

If someone is copying you, let him or her know. Tell them that under the law, you are entitled to their profits. They might not even know they are copying you.

Promotion

Pick up newspapers at every show you do and take one home with you. Next year, send them a press release. People will come up to your booth and say they saw you in the paper.

A press release is one or two pages of information that tells who, what, where, why, when, etc. Write "For Immediate Release" at the top, then put your contact information. Explain why your method or style of craftsmanship is unique or what you are doing to save the planet. A press release is always double-spaced.

Include a cover letter with your press release. Tell the editor why his readers need to know about you. Also include a glossy black-and-white 5x7 or 8x10 photograph of you and your shop and a photograph of your craft. You should take the photos in color in case you ever need color, then print them in black and white. (You can't print color from a black and white photo.) Never write on the back of a publicity photo. It can't be reproduced, as the writing will show through. Write or use a rubber stamp on a label, then put the label on the back of the photo.

Microsoft Publisher is very useful for artist statements, postcards, stationery, catalogs, brochures, hang tags, etc. Some online printers such as www.printing4less.com can use your uploaded Publisher files. There is a Publisher lesson in this book.

Use first class mail for mailing your cards and brochures. Bulk mail only saves you about ten cents a letter and it is less likely to be read. After you spend $125 for a bulk mail application, $125 for an annual fee, and all the time to separate your mail by zip code, have you really saved any money? Bulk mail rates are at www.usps.com/directmail/

Pricing

Pricing is one of the biggest problems for beginners. Everything has a "right price," regardless of who you are selling it to. There is a pricing form in the computer section of this book. Pricing is simply adding the cost of materials in each piece to the labor cost (how many hours to make it times how much you want to make an hour), then multiplying by 2.5 for your retail price. Wholesale is half of that. At a craft fair, your discount from the retail price may make the difference whether you make a profit at that show or not.

Never under-price your work. You might make more sales, but you will be broke at the end of the year. Never reduce your price unless you can cut your costs (both materials and labor). Selling out at a show is not always a good thing. If your product sells out at a show the first day, it is priced too low.

Find your best market. If your product price is too high for your market, find another market. Sell your one-of-a-kind pieces through a craft gallery, where your product is not compared to products at Target or Wal-Mart.

Have multiple price points. If you have products priced for low income, middle income, and high-end customers, you will always make money at a show.

Put price stickers on every product you have for sale. You don't want the customer to think you are making up the price while you try to remember what it is. And, you won't waste the time of a customer who cant afford the item.

Set business hours for your home business. Self-discipline is the hardest part of being self-employed. Find out what wastes time. Use a message machine that says you are in the shop when you are working, so you won't be disturbed.

5 ways to increase profits

1. Increase the price. If your product has the right price (see above), you can only raise your price if you improve the product. Many crafts at fairs are priced too low. If your price seems too high for the customers who visit your booth, then you simply have to find a show with more affluent customers.

2. Reduce material costs. Find a way to get your materials for less money. The Internet is great for this. Create less waste. Buying too many materials, or throwing away scraps that could be sold, add up to increased costs.

3. Increase production. Either work faster or make more products at a time, or both.

4. Make more sales. Do more shows, better shows, or make additional sales to other outlets.

5. Reduce overhead. Turn off the lights when you go out. One good helper is better than two not-good helpers. Keep the entire business production in your garage.

Miscellaneous

Write down where you want to be financially in 3 months, 1 year, and 5 years. The simple act of writing it down programs the subconscious to take actions that help you with your goals. This really works!

Test market every new product. Don't make a hundred of one design until you have sold a few. Craft fairs and wholesale trade shows are very helpful for product research.

Write down a goal for production each day. You can do this last thing in the evening before, or first thing in the morning.

Save 10% of the gross from every show. This adds up. Don't spend it on anything unless it is a house or retirement.

Computers and Microsoft™ Office

Introduction

If you have a computer with Microsoft Excel, you can price your crafts, organize your shows, and keep a customer mailing list with the spreadsheets we have included in this book.

You probably don't have enough time between doing shows and making products to wade through a lot of thick books about Microsoft **Office** or computers in general, I have provided a few simple solutions. This section includes:

1. A basic beginner lesson for using **Windows** and **Excel.**
2. 8 ready-made spreadsheet templates.
3. Tips for using computers and software.

If you are totally new to computers, I recommend you try sitting at the computer with a friend who has some experience. You can learn more about **Windows** in one hour that way than in 10 hours reading a book about computers.

Hopefully you already have Microsoft **Office** installed on your computer. If you don't, **Office** comes with a user's guide to tell you how to install the software.

I have included a basic **Excel** lesson, which, if you need it and you follow the directions carefully, will get you started using spreadsheets. The design work has already been done for you. Once you learn how to use and change the spreadsheets and forms I have provided, you will be able to create your own spreadsheets if you need to.

How to use Microsoft Excel

You don't have to learn much about Excel to use the spreadsheets in this book. If you follow these instructions one time the spreadsheets will be easy.

Start **Excel** by clicking on the Start button, point to Programs, and then click Microsoft **Excel**. Or click on **Excel** on the **Office** Shortcut bar if you have one. If the spreadsheet does not fill the screen, click on the middle (Maximize) box in the upper right corner.
Place your cursor on the cell A1. A is on the top row, 1 is a number to the left. Type "5" (don't type the quotation marks). Press enter.
Place the cursor on B and left click. Type "6". Press enter.
Use the right arrow key to go to cell C1 (or move the cursor, then left click). Type "+A1+B1" (without the quotation marks), then press the enter key. The number 11 will now be in cell C1.
Place the cursor on A1 again, and type "3". Press enter. The number 9 will appear in cell C1. The formula in C1 adds the numbers in A1 and B1.
Place the cursor on D1. Type "+sum(a1:c1)", then press enter (make sure it is a colon, not a semicolon.) The number 18 will appear in D1. The sum function in this formula added the numbers in A1, B1, and C1.
Place the cursor on E1. Type "+(A1*D1)", then press enter. The number 54 will appear in E1. The formula reads the * (asterisk) as a multiply command.
Place the cursor in B1. Type "4". Press enter. Now the number in C1 changes to 7 (the formula in C1 adds A1 plus B1). The number in D1 changes to 14, and the number in E1 changes to 42 (A1 multiplied by B1).
Select or highlight cells A1 through D1 by placing the cursor on A1 and holding down the left mouse button as you drag the cursor over B1, C1, and D1. Then select Format>Cells. Click on Alignment; click on the down arrow next to the horizontal box for more choices. Click on Center. Now the numbers are centered in their cells.
Select Format>Cells, then Number and Currency. Click on Okay. Now the numbers will have dollar signs in front of them. To get rid of the zeros to the right of the decimal place, change decimal places where you selected Currency to 0 by clicking on the arrows.
Put the cursor on A1. Select Insert>Rows. Now A1 is empty. Type "March". Move the cursor to B1 and type "April". Move the cursor to C1 and type Total. Press enter, then highlight A1, B1, C1 and click on the Bold Button.
To save this spreadsheet, click on File>Save As. Type a name in the file box, and click the Save button. To print this spreadsheet, chose File>Print

Downloading Spreadsheets

- All of the following spreadsheets and forms can be opened and downloaded at www.craftmasters.com/templates.htm. (They can also be purchased on a CD-Rom, see last page.)

- Just click on the spreadsheet to open it. Excel (if you have it on your computer) will start and the spreadsheet will appear on your screen. If it is password protected, the password is "handmade." You can also chose to save or download it to your computer and open it later while running Excel.

Using the Spreadsheets

1. Click on the filename of the spreadsheet you wish to use. When you click on an .xls spreadsheet, **Excel** will automatically start.
2. You can start Excel first, then open a spreadsheet by clicking on File>Open...from the drop down menu, then finding the spreadsheet.
3. Click on the yellow file folder with the left arrow, until you see Drive C in the window.
4. The examples in this book demonstrates what the form is designed to do and shows you, by example, where to insert your own information. All of the formulas are already in place on the form. To see what they look like, click on the cell, and the formula will appear in the contents window. Don't change the formula.
5. Save the document file with your info under a new file name using the File>Save As command. Save the document file in a different folder (the My Documents folder will work nicely.) This will ensure that any modifications you make will not alter the original form or any other forms you might have open. For the new file name, use a name you can easily remember, such as my prices, 2008 deadlines, 2008 calendar, the name of the customer, etc.
6. Fill in the form using the instructions in this book and save again (using the File>Save command this time, not Save As). Enter data in green or black rectangles. Results (calculations) will appear in red rectangles. Don't enter data in red rectangles! That is where the formulas are. If you accidentally type over a formula in a red rectangle, you can start over by reloading the spreadsheet from your original directory, disk, or online.
7. Print the form using either the print tool Icon or the File>Print command.

Craft Fairs at a Glance (fair year.xls)

This form shows the fairs for an entire year at a glance, and alerts you to weeks when you don't have a fair. This form is very useful in showing the big picture and helping you get organized.

Step-by-step instructions:

1. Print out this form and tape it up in a conspicuous place.
2. Write in names and dates of all fairs you are considering doing. Write in the dates and name of a fair when you get the application, if you haven't already. You don't need to write the entire name of the fair, just enough so you know which fair it is.
3. When you have some extra time, open this form in the computer and enter the names you had hand written on the previous printed form. Print this out to have a neat yearly calendar of all of your fairs. Indicate any fairs you are accepted in with Bold Type. To do this on the computer, highlight the name of the fair you typed in, then click on the **B** button in the button bar at the top of the page.
4. You can designate fairs applied to but not accepted yet with a question mark (?), fairs you are on the waiting list for with a "w", fairs that you are considering but haven't yet applied for with parenthesis ( ), and fairs you are in with **bold** type.

	A	B	C	D	E	F	G	H	I	J	K
1	**Craft Fairs at a Glance**			For:		Year:					
2	Month	Date	1st Weekend	Date	2nd Weekend	Date	3rd Weekend	Date	4th Weekend	Date	5th Weekend
3											
4	Jan.										
5											
6	Feb.							24-26	Fountain Hills		
7											
8	March										
9											
10	April										
11											
12	May										
13											
14	June			**8-12**	**Three Rivers**						
15											
16	July							20-23	AnnArbor		
17											
18	Aug.	3-4	Park City								
19											
20	Sept.										
21											
22	Oct.										
23											
24	Nov.										
25											
26	Dec.										
27	Notes:										
28											
29	**Bold type indicates Accepted.**			Normal type indicates applied for			( ) indicates "considering, not applied yet".				

Craft Pricing (pricing.xls)

Use this form to automatically calculate the price of your craft product. It is very simple and useful. Discount and Markup calculators are also included.

Step-by-step instructions:

1. Enter your numbers in column F only. Results appear in column G.
2. Calculate how many pieces you can make in a day. Put that number in the first box. If you take two days to make a piece, put .5 in this box. If you can make 50 pieces from start to finish, put 50 in this box. The spreadsheet will divide this number by 8 to determine how many you make in an hour.
3. Next you enter the salary you want to make a year. Be realistic here. Somewhere between a teacher and a doctor, depending on what you really expect to be able to make. If you have been doing this for a while, enter the amount you made last year. The spreadsheet will divide this number by 1920, which is the number of hours in a working year with 40 hour weeks and 4 weeks off for vacation as a basis.
4. Now you enter the total cost of the materials in each piece. For a woodworker, for example, this would be the wood plus any mechanical parts. Press enter.

The spreadsheet will now calculate your hourly rate, divide it by the pieces per hour, and add materials cost. It will add 15% for overhead, 10% for profit, and show the results in the box next to Distributor price (G7). This is your absolute minimum price for the craft product, out the door of your shop.

The wholesale price is the absolute minimum price plus 15% for a sales rep or other costs of getting your work into a retail store, such as mailing brochures or selling at wholesale trade shows.

The retail price is the wholesale price times 2, which would be the price you sell it at a craft show or the price a store would normally sell it for.

When entering a percent number in the Discounts and Markups section, always use a decimal first. For example, enter .40, not 40 for percent discount in F15.

	A	B	C	D	E	F	G
1					**Craft Pricing**		
2							
3							
4	Number of pieces you can complete per day:					40	
5	Amount of salary you want to make per year:					$75,000	
6			Cost of materials per piece:			$3.20	Results:
7						Distributor price:	$13.77
8						Wholesale price:	$15.83
9						Retail price:	$31.66
10							
11							
12					**Discounts**		
13							
14				Original price of item:		$39.00	
15				Percent discount:		40%	
16						Sale price:	$23.40
17						Amount of discount:	$15.60
18							
19				Original price of item:		$39.00	
20				Sale price:		$25.00	
21						Amount of discount:	$14.00
22						Percent discount:	36%
23							
24					**Markups**		
25							
26				Cost of item:		$19.00	
27				Percent markup:		110%	
28						Markup is:	$20.90
29						Selling price is:	$39.90
30							
31				Selling price of item:		$39.00	
32				Cost of item:		$19.00	
33						Percent markup is:	105%
34							
35				Selling price of item:		$39.00	
36				Percent markup:		125%	
37						Cost of item:	$17.33
38							
39							

Craft Fair Application Organizer (organizer.xls)

The purpose of this form is to avoid missing application deadlines. When the information you input is sorted by the computer, you will have a list of upcoming deadline dates in the correct order.

Step-by-step instructions:

1. When you receive a brochure or application for a fair in the mail, immediately enter the fair name and deadline information on a printout of this form as shown. You don't have to boot up the computer each time, though. Write the fair information on this form by hand, and every two weeks or so, enter and sort the information on your computer, and print a new updated form. Keep this form in plain sight (not in a drawer!) on the refrigerator or bulletin board where you will see it often to check for approaching deadlines.
2. Enter deadline dates in column C. You don't have to type in the whole date. You can type au 10 and the computer will insert August 10 for you because the column is already formatted to show dates. Type the actual show dates in Column D, July 3-7, for example.
3. Check whether you need photos or slides. The time to check whether the show requires a photo of your booth, or a workshop slide, is when you first get the application. When the deadline is tomorrow, you may not have enough time.
4. After you have put in all of the fairs you are considering, sort the list by the deadline date. To do this, highlight the entire list that you want to sort by dragging the cursor from the upper left of the first entry to the lower right of the last entry. The click on Data>sort, then select deadline (or column C) in the sort by box, and click on the ascending button. Print out the form and post it where you will see it.
5. After entering the information on this form from the application, file the application in the folder for the month the fair takes place. When you apply to the fair, cross it off of this list.
6. When you find out that you are accepted, enter the fair in bold letters on the "Craft Fairs at a Glance" form on the next page.
7. The total of the upcoming show fees is shown at G38.
8. Change headings and columns as needed. Change the heading for Promoter to Motel Reservations, Income, or anything else you would like to note about the fair. You can delete a column by right clicking on the letter at the top of the column and selecting Delete.

	A	B	C	D	E	F	G	H
1			**Craft Fair Organizer**					
2					Photos or	Applied		Accepted?
3	Fair	Promoter	Deadline	Date	Slides	for? y/n	Show Fee	(y/n)
4	Park City	Kimball	2/4/2006	August 3-4	Slides	y	$350	y
5	Ann Arbor	State St.	2/28/2006	July 20-23	Slides	n	$450	
6								
7								
8								
9								
10								
11								
12								
13								
14								
15								
16								
17								
18								
19								
20								
21								
22								
23								
24								
25								
26								
27								
28								
29								
30								
31								
32								
33								
34								
35								
36								
37								
38							$800	

Spreadsheet Tip

Do you have unexplained information In Excel cells? If a spreadsheet cell shows #####, it means that the cell is not wide enough to show the whole number. You can select the cell, click Format>Cells, Number to change the way the number is formatted. Or you can use Format>Column, Autofit Selection to adjust the column's width. Or you could just use the mouse, click on the line at the right top of the column, and drag to make the column wider.

Craft Show Expense Report (expenses.xls)

This form will show you how much you really make at a craft fair. It will also help you record business trip expenses for later deduction on your Schedule C at tax time. There are limits on the deductions allowable for costs of meals and transportation.

Generally you must be away from your hometown to deduct travel expenses on business trips. Craft fairs and trade shows are considered temporary business locations and your necessary expenses in getting to and from the fairs are considered business expenses and not commuting expenses (which are not deductible). You must keep records and receipts to support your deduction of these expenses.

The following expenses of a business trip away from home are deductible:
Plane, railroad, taxi and other transportation fares
Hotel and lodging expenses
Meal costs (50%)
Tips, telephone, and fax costs
Laundry and cleaning expenses
Excess baggage charges (including insurance)

Your tax home is your place of business, regardless of where you maintain your family residence. This tax home includes the entire city or general area of your business premises. Your residence may be your tax home if your income is dependent on craft fairs at widely scattered locations, you have no other fixed place of work, and your residence is in a location economically suited for your work.

Step-by-step instructions:

1. Enter your headings as shown and enter your physical location for each day in row 7 (traveling to or from, or at show).
2. Enter all expenses for the show as shown. Enter booth fee or deposit in B29, and put commission paid (if any) in row 29.
3. Net income shown at I33 is equal to show income minus expenses and show fees.
4. In this example the show fee is shown on Wednesday and the 20% commission given to the promoter at the end of the show is shown on Friday.
5. This form is set up for a weekend craft fair. For a trade show during the week, change the days of the week at the top to begin with Sunday instead of Wednesday.

	A	B	C	D	E	F	G	H	I
1				**Show Expense Report**					
2									
3			Show Name:	Tempe		Artist:			
4			Starting Date:	4/1/2006		Ending Date:	4/3/2006		
5			Comments:						
6	Date	Wednesday	Thursday	Friday	Saturday	Sunday	Monday	Tuesday	Totals
7	Location								
8	Lodging		$32.00	$32.00	$32.00	$32.00			$128.00
9	Breakfast			$5.40	$6.30	$3.95			$15.65
10	Lunch			$3.00	$3.50	$6.00			$12.50
11	Dinner			$11.50	$18.00	$7.40			$36.90
12	Phone								$0.00
13	Laundry								$0.00
14	Baggage								$0.00
15	**Sub-totals**	**$0.00**	**$32.00**	**$51.90**	**$59.80**	**$49.35**	**$0.00**	**$0.00**	$193.05
16	Airfare								$0.00
17	Train								$0.00
18	Cab								$0.00
19	Tips								$0.00
20	**Sub-totals**	**$0.00**	**$0.00**	**$0.00**	**$0.00**	**$0.00**	**$0.00**	**$0.00**	$0.00
21	Gas/Oil		$105.00				$121.00		$226.00
22	Parking			$15.00	$15.00	$15.00			$45.00
23	Tolls								$0.00
24	Rentals								$0.00
25	**Sub-total**	**$0.00**	**$105.00**	**$15.00**	**$15.00**	**$15.00**	**$121.00**	**$0.00**	$271.00
26									
27	Total Exp.	**$0.00**	**$137.00**	**$66.90**	**$74.80**	**$64.35**	**$121.00**	**$0.00**	$464.05
28									
29	Show Fees	$550.00							$550.00
30									
31	Show Sales			$521	$794	$336			$1,651
32									
33	Signature:							**Net Income from Show**	**$636.95**

Craft Fair Equipment List (equipment.xls)

Use this list to keep track of what to bring to a craft fair. It will certainly dampen your spirits to drive 500 miles to do a fair and discover that you have left something important behind. Glance over this list again before leaving for every fair.

Step-by-step instructions:

1. Change or delete any of the items in column A just by typing over them. Add other items as needed, such as different displays, kinds of stock, etc.
2. Print out a copy of this form, with the "Packed" and "Need" columns either filled out or blank, to be filled in by hand.

If you are interested in the value of what you have or need to get, or for planning or insurance purposes, insert the value in the Cost columns. The combined totals will appear in I35.

	A	B	C	D	E	F	G	H	I
1				Craft Fair Equipment List					
2									
3	Item	Packed	Need	Cost		Item	Packed	Need	Cost
4	Canopy	x				Stock	x		
5	Walls or Backdrop	x				Calculator	x		
6	Stakes	x				Sales Tax Certificate			
7	Weights					Tax Chart			
8	Banner					Receipt Book			
9	Tables	x				Pens			
10	Chairs	x				Charge Machine	x		
11	Table Cloths	x				Charge Slips	x		
12	Display Cases	x				Bags			
13	Display Boards	x				Change			
14	Duct Tape		x	$4.00		Price tags			
15	Hammer					Business Cards	x		
16	Screwdriver	x				Brochures			
17	Pliers					Signs (pre-made)			
18	C-Clamps	x				Marker	x		
19	Push-pins					Sign materials			
20	Nails					Mailing List Book			
21	Safety-pins					Hang Tags	x		
22	Glue					Order Forms			
23	Extension Cord	x				Cooler	x		
24	Lighting					Thermos			
25	Extra Bulbs					Food			
26	First Aid Kit	x				Snacks			
27	Fire Extinguisher					Fair Information			
28	Fire Retardant Cert.					Parking pass			
29	Bungee Cords					State Map			
30	Rope	x				Fair Map			
31	Mirror								
32									
33				$4.00					$0.00
34									
35							Total Value		$4.00

Customer Mailing List (customer.xls)

This is a list of your current and past customers. All you do is enter the address from every check that you get at a craft fair or show. In addition you can use a guest book to get addresses. You have the customers enter their name and address whenever they buy something using a credit card or cash instead of a check.

Your list should consist of actual satisfied customers who know your work. Notify them of new products and upcoming craft fairs where they can buy from you. When you send them a brochure, ask them to pass it along to someone they know who might like to buy your products.

Step-by-step instructions:

1. In **Excel**, open customer.xls. Select Data>Form to see the database format. Enter information as shown. If you don't need information in a specific blank, just skip it.
2. Use the Tab key to move from field to field.
3. Use Enter or arrow keys to move to the next record.
4. The example shown on the next page is for the database view in **Excel**.
5. To print labels, use the envelopes and labels function in **Word**. (See below for information how to do this).

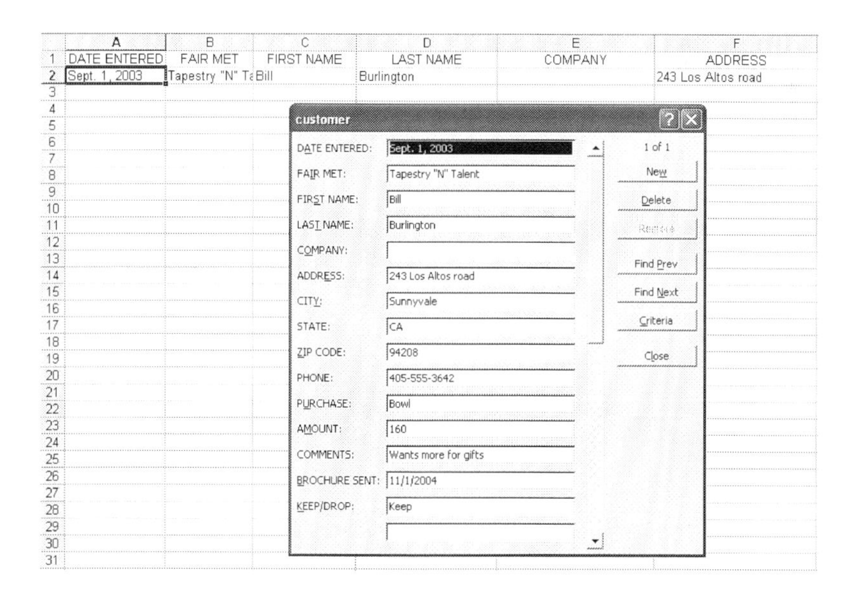

How to print mailing labels in Microsoft Word:

1. Open Word, select Tools, Mail Merge.
2. Under 1. Main Document, click on Create, Mailing Labels, Active window.
3. Under 2, Data Source, Get Data, Open Data Source.
4. In the Open Data Source window, select Files of type (at the bottom)—MS Excel Worksheets (*.xls). Then browse file up or down to find your top1100galleries.xls and open it. Ignore the first window that says something about asap utilities (click OK), then in the little Microsoft Excel window, select Database.
5. A window opens that says Set up main document.
6. Select Avery standard, then select 5160 address labels. Click okay.
7. In the Create Labels window that opens, click on Insert Merge Field, and put the name on the first line.
8. Press enter to go to the next line and click on insert merge field again and put the address on the second line. Put the city, state and zip on the third line.

Click okay, then click on #. Merge. In the Merge window that opens, click on All, then Merge again. Your labels will appear. Put in mail label (1x2 5/8 paper 5160 and print your labels.

More Mail List Tips

How to sort your mail list in an Excel database

To sort data, click Data>Sort. A dialog box will pop up, letting you specify how you want the data sorted. You can sort up to three levels. Select the first field you want to sort by and select Ascending order. Make sure the Header Row button is selected. To perform a more complex sort, select the criteria to sort by for the second and third levels. For example, if first and last names are different fields in your database, you may want to first sort by last name and then by first name in case some records have the same last name.

Filtering your database

If you want all of the names from a specific ZIP code or city, use AutoFilter to filter out unwanted records, leaving a list of those you want. The rest of the records are hidden from view. You can save the filtered database under a new name, without altering the first database. Choose Data>AutoFilter and an arrow appears at the top of each column in your database. Click on the arrow and a drop-down list displays all of the values that appear in that field. Chose Custom to specify values equal to what you want.

How to use Microsoft Word to print a sheet of return address labels

Using the Label function in **Word**, you can print an entire sheet of the same label to create return address labels. Select Tools>Envelopes and Labels, then Labels, then Options. Select Avery standard and select 5160-Address for the Product number. Click OK, Type in your return address in the Address: Box. Click on New Document, and print as many pages as you need.

How to Make an Artist Statement

An Artist Statement is written by the craftsperson to describe the work that he or she has created. Art shows and craft fairs often request that the craftsperson display an artist's statement in their booth for the public to read. The statement tells the customer (and sometimes the show promoters) a little more about the craft than is obvious in the presentation. Sometimes the craftsperson will learn more about his motives by writing the statement.

Writing your own statement is not that hard. Just answer the following questions in one page, and you will have your own artist's statement.

1. Why do you work with the medium or process you have chosen.
2. How many people help you create your work?
3. Is there a central theme or interest from which you generate your work?
4. Is there symbolism in your work?
5. Are there contemporary or historical images or crafts that you are influenced by?
6. Are you trying to invoke an emotion or stimulate the intellect of the user/viewer?
7. What associations do you hope viewers make when viewing your work?
8. What formal aspects interest you? Color? Line? Value? Shape? Form? Movement? Function?

The statement should be 8 ½" by 11." It should have your photo and your name and address at the top, along with your email and website. There are some sample artist statements at
http://www.naia-artists.org/work/statement2.htm

Reveille by John C. Reiger

Alive again! an' ready to show
Winter's over I'm rarin' to go

Goodby to the boredom dull staring at walls
Now I am Faire-bound off to the Malls.

Ol' Bertha is flying past princes and prole's
Filled to the sunroof with pitchers and bowls

So scatter before me you freeway turtles
I am a Red Streak bounding hurdles.

Friends and Fortune beckon ahead.
Bright lights, warm smiles, and plenty of bread.

I come once again to hear the praise,
Puffs, and purchases for three or four days.

Unless, of course the show's for the birds,
And all that attend are lookers and nerds.

But it's my life this "Doing the shows."
How I survive it, nobody knows.

"Hope springs eternal" so optimists say.
I guess I agree, I welcome today.

Top Craft Fairs

How to get applications

When sending for craft fair applications, first select the desirable fairs from your craft fair list or guides. Write the addresses on #10 business envelopes. I recommend writing the shows instead of calling them. Many shows do not have a full time staff member to answer phones. In addition, they might get your address wrong over the phone.

Download this letter from www.craftmasters.com/spreadsheets.htm. Put your name and mailing address at the top. Add or delete questions from this letter as desired, then date and sign it. Make as many copies as you have address labels or addressed envelopes for.

Letter to fair promoter for application (fairletter.doc)

Craft Fair Application Request

Date_____________

Dear Craft Fair Organizer:

Please forward an application and any other information about your upcoming show. I would also like to be placed on your mailing list for future shows.

If the following information is not included with your application, please write the answers on this letter and return it with the application.

- Do you provide or assist in canopy and table rental for this show?
- Are there nearby areas for self-contained RV parking?
- Do you allow amplified music in close proximity to the artists to the extent that they cannot converse with their customers without raising their voice?
- Do you give artists who demonstrate their craft preference in the jurying process?
- How many people attended the show last year?

Sincerely, _________________________

How to organize your fair applications.

1. Get 12 file folders. Write the name of a month on each one. 12 folders, 12 months.
2. When you get each application, write down the show name, show date, and deadline date on the craft fair organizer on page 87.
3. Write the show and show date on the fair calendar on page 89.
4. File the applications in the file folder for the month the show is held.

The following list consist of the best shows in the country. Exact show dates and deadline dates are not shown, because these change yearly. When you write one of these shows and ask for information, they will send you an application with the correct dates at no charge. Then you will have the exact dates of the show every year, and much more information than any guide can give you.

You may do better or worse at any of the shows listed here then I do. I do not guarantee any of them, but after you do a few of them you will find that they are better than most. The ratings are there to give you a general idea of the better shows, but all of the shows on this list are above average. The inclusion of ratings for specific shows is based on word of mouth, magazine articles, attendance, years show has been in business, and personal experience.

It seems that at nearly every show I do, whether it is a well-known show or not, the craftsperson or artist on one side will take in much more money than I do, and the person on the other side will not do nearly as well.

The names and addresses listed here were accurate at the time this book went to print. Addresses and phone numbers change. If you get your letter back, google that fair to get their new address. Please let us know about any bad addresses. Just send an email info@craftmastersguild.com I republish this book every year, and try to keep it up to date.

May you get into at least half of the shows you apply to
And may you make twice as much money as you expected to.

ST	CRAFT FAIR	ATT	Mon	ADD	CITY	ST	ZIP	PH	Rt
AL	Christmas Village Festival	45,000	Nov	P. O. Box 101441	Birming-ham	AL	35210	205-836-7178	A
AL	NEACA Fall Show	30,000	Sep	P. O. Box 1113 W. Station	Huntsville	AL	35805	205-274-7918	A
AL	Mobile Bay Fest	200,000	Oct	P. O. Box 1827	Mobile	AL	36633	251-470-7730	A-
AL	Kentuck Festival of the Arts	32,000	Oct	503 Main Avenue	Northport	AL	35476	205-758-1257	A-
AL	National Shrimp Festival	200,000	Oct	P. O. Box 3869	Gulf Shores	AL	36547	251-968-6904	A+
AL	Alabama Blueberry Festival	25,000	Jun	1010-B Douglas Avenue	Brewton	AL	36426	251-867-3224	B
AL	Fairhope Arts and Crafts Festival	180,000	Mar	P. O. Drawer 10	Daphne	AL	36526	334-621-8222	B
AL	Foley Art in the Park	35,000	May	119 West Laurel Avenue	Foley	AL	36535	251-943-4381	B
AL	Hartselle Depot Days	15,000	Sep	P. O. Box 817	Hartselle	AL	35640	256-773-4370	B
AL	Delta Zone Market Place	15,000	Nov	P. O. Box 18696	Huntsville	AL	35804	256-894-0117	B
AL	Panoply	85,000	Apr	700 Monroe St., Ste 2	Huntsville	AL	35802	256-519-2787	B
AL	Montgomery Fest. in the Park	13,000	Oct	1010 Forest Avenue	Montgom-ery	AL	36106	334-241-2300	B
AL	Festival in the Park	19,000	Oct	1010 Forest Avenue	Montgom-ery	AL	36106	334-241-2300	B
AL	Homestead Hollow Christmas	13,000	Nov	P. O. Box 190	Springville	AL	35146	205-836-8483	B

AL	Homestead Hollow Harvest	18,000	Oct	P. O. Box 190	Springville	AL	35146	205-836-8483	B
AL	Christmas on the Coosa	20,000	Dec	P. O. Box 936	Wetumpka	AL	36092	334-567-1313	B
AR	Applegate Place A&C Fest.	200,000	Oct	P. O. Box 1041	Bentonville	AR	72712	479-273-7478	A
AR	Arts & Carafts Festival	35,000	Oct	P. O. Box 5009	Bella Vista	AR	72714	479-855-2064	A-
AR	War Eagle Fair	195,000	Oct	11036 High Sky	Hindsville	AR	72738	479-789-5398	A+
AR	Mountain View Folkfest	60,000	Apr	2926 Highway 150	Blytheville	AR	72560	870-763-5512	B
AR	Beanfest	60,000	Oct	2926 Highway 150	Blytheville	AR	72560	888-679-2859	B
AR	Toad Suck Daze	155,000	Apr	900 Oak Street	Conway	AZ	72032	501-327-7788	B
AR	Hillbilly Corner Arts, Craft	25,000	May	22530 Deer Run Rd.	Hindsville	AR	72738	479-789-5685	B
AR	Arkansas Apple Festival	45,000	Oct	P. O. Box 382	Lincoln	AR	72744	479-267-3916	B
AR	Springdale Fall Craft Fest	20,000	Oct	5557 Walden Street	Lowell	AR	72745	479-756-2979	B
AR	Old Timer's Days	40,000	May	P. O. Box 245	Van Buren	OR	72957	501-474-8322	B
AR	Jonquil Festival	15,000	Mar	P. O. Box 98	Washington	AR	71862	870-983-2684	B
AR	Autumn Arts and Craft Show	15,000	Oct	P. O. Box 1041	Bentonville	AR	72712	479-273-7478	B
AZ	Fine Arts and Wine Festival		Mar	15648 N. Eagles Nest Dr.	Fountain Hills	AZ	85268	480-837-5637	A
AZ	Fountain Hills Great Fair	150,000	Nov	P O Box 17598	Fountain Hills	AZ	85269	602-837-1654	A

AZ	4th Avenue Street Fair (Spring)	300,000	Mar	329 E 7th	Tucson	AZ	85705	800-933-2477	A
AZ	Carefree Fine Art & Wine Festival	40,000	Nov	15648 N. Eagles Nest Dr.	Fountain Hills	AZ	85268	480-837-5637	A-
AZ	Sedona Arts Festival	5,000	Oct	P. O. Box 2729	Sedona	AZ	86339	928-204-9456	A-
AZ	Art in the Park	10,000	Oct	P. O. Box 247	Sierra Vista	AZ	85636	520-378-1763	A-
AZ	Tempe Fall Festival of the Arts	230,000	Dec	520 S. Mill Ave. Ste. 201	Tempe	AZ	85281	480-967-4877	A-
AZ	Tempe Spring Festival of the Arts	300,000	Mar	520 S. Mill Ave., Ste. 201	Tempe	AZ	85281	602-967-4877	A-
AZ	Fourth Avenue Street Fair	325,000	Dec	329 East Seventh Street	Tucson	AZ	85705	520-624-5004	A-
AZ	Desert Festival of Fine Arts	40,000	Aug	15648 North Eagles Nest Dr.	Fountain Hills	AZ	85268	480-837-5637	A+
AZ	Peoria Stadium Fall Fest. Of A and C	10,000	Nov	P. O. Box 1803	Cave Creek	AZ	85327	480-488-2014	B
AZ	Glendale Chocolate Affaire	75,000	Feb	5850 West Glendale Ave.	Glendale	AZ	85301	623-930-2959	B
AZ	Patagonia Fall Festival	15,000	Oct	P. O. Box 241	Patagonia	AZ	85624	520-394-0060	B
AZ	Prescott Courthouse Plaza A and C	15,000	July	4196 Coburn	Prescott	AZ	86392	928-771-1498	B
AZ	Sierra Vista Art in the Park	20,000	Oct	P. O. Box 247	Sierra Vista	AZ	85636	520-378-1763	B
AZ	Artfest of Fifth Avenue	22,000	Oct	P. O. Box 328	Tempe	AZ	85280	480-968-5353	B

AZ	Yuma Christmas Craft Fest.	20,000	Dec	180 First Street Ste C	Yuma	AZ	85364	928-782-5712	B
CA	Art Affair	9,000	Oct	3051 Via Maderas	Altadena	CA	91001	818-797-6803	A
CA	Contemporary Craft Market	11,000	Jun	575 Cooke St. A2820	Honolulu	HI	96813	808-422-7362	A
CA	Contemporary Craft Market	12,000	Nov	575 Cooke St A2820	Honolulu	HI	96813	808-422-7362	A
CA	Sawdust Festival	200,000	Jul Aug	935 Laguna Canyon	Laguna Beach	CA	92651	949-494-3030	A
CA	Mill Valley Fall Arts Festival	15,000	Sep	P O Box 300	Mill Valley	CA	94942	415-381-0525	A
CA	Rotary Art Show	30,000	May	P. O. Box 2215	Saratoga	CA	95070	408-725-2434	A
CA	Palo Alto Festival of the Arts	25,000	Aug	1384 Weston Road	Scotts Valley	CA	95066	831-438-4751	A
CA	KPFA Holidays Crafts Fair	10,000	Dec	1929 Mlk Jr Way	Berkeley	CA	94704	510-848-6767	A-
CA	Affaire in the Gardens (Fall)	60,000	Oct	8400 Gregory Way	Beverly Hills	CA	90211	310-550-4628	A-
CA	Avocado Festival	110,000	Oct	P. O. Box 146	Carpenteria	CA	93014	805-684-0038	A-
CA	La Quinta Arts Festival	25,000	Mar	P O Box 777	La Quinta	CA	92253	760-564-1244	A-
CA	Winter Fantasy Laguna Beach	20,000	Nov	935 Laguna Canyon Road	Laguna Beach	CA	92651	949-494-3030	A-
CA	Museum of Art Artists Market	4,000	Jun	2300 East Ocean	Long Beach	CA	90803	310-439-2119	A-
CA	Labor Day Festival	15,000	Aug	P. O. Box 56	Mammoth Lakes	CA	93546	760-873-7042	A-

CA	Harvest Festival	30,000	Nov	601 N. Mcdowell	Petaluma	CA	94954	707-778-6300	A-
CA	Strawberry Festival	65,000	May	P O Box 280	Pine Grove	CA	95665	209-296-1195	A-
CA	Fiesta Hermosa Arts & Crafts	150,000	May	1926 S. Pc Hwy #109-B	Redondo Beach	CA	90501	310-316-0951	A-
CA	Tapestry in Talent	75,000	Aug	255 N. Market St #124	San Jose	CA	95110	408-494-3490	A-
CA	Connois-seur's Market Place	80,000	July	1384 Weston Road	Scotts Valley	CA	95066	831-438-4751	A-
CA	Celebration Of Crafts-women	10,000	Nov	3453 18th Street	San Francisco	CA	94110	415-431-1180	A-
CA	Festival of the Arts	17,000	Sep	4130 La Jolla Vil. Dr.7	La Jolla	CA	92037	619-456-1268	A+
CA	Sausalito Arts Festival	50,000	Aug	P O Box 10	Sausalito	CA	94966	415-332-3555	A+
CA	Kings Mountain Art Fair	20,000	Sep	13106 Skyline Boule-vard	Woodside	CA	94062	650-851-2710	A+
CA	Cupertino Rotary Octfest	30,000	Oct	P. O. Box 1343	Alameda	CA	94501	510-865-3636	B
CA	North Country Fair and Harvest	10,000	Sep	P. O. Box 664	Arcata	CA	95518	707-822-5320	B
CA	Live Oak Park Fair	5,000	Jun	P O Box 9188	Berkeley	CA	94709	510-526-7363	B
CA	Boulder Creek Art and Wine Fest.		May	12805 Highway 9	Boulder	CA	95006	831-338-2578	B
CA	Burlingame Art in the Park	35,000	Jun	P. O. Box 1963	Burlin-game	CA	94011	650-348-7699	B
CA	Los Gatos Fiesta De Artes	30,000	Aug	P. O. Box 1963	Burlin-game	CA	94011	650-348-7699	B

CA	Downtown Burbank Fine Arts	15,000	Nov	P. O. Box 4389	Chats-worth	CA	91311	818-709-2907	B
CA	Warner Park Fine Art/Crafts	15,000	Nov	P. O. Box 4389	Chats-worth	CA	91311	818-709-2907	B
CA	Desert Arts Festival, Palm Springs	15,000	Dec	P. O. Box 4389	Chats-worth	CA	91311	818-709-2907	B
CA	Village Arts Festival	30,000	Nov	P. O. Box 4389	Chats-worth	CA	91311	818-709-2907	B
CA	Village Venture A and C Faire	20,000	Oct	205 Yale Avenue	Claremont	CA	91711	909-624-1681	B
CA	Riverside Dickens Festival	25,000	Feb	P. O. Box 1959	Corona	CA	92879	909-735-0101	B
CA	Courtland Pear Fair	15,000	July	P. O. Box 492	Courtland	CA	95615	916-775-2000	B
CA	Whole Earth Festival	20,000	May	260 S. Silo	Davis	CA	95616	916-752-2569	B
CA	Fairfield Tomato Festival	45,000	Aug	1000 Texas St. #D	Fairfield	CA	94533	707-422-0103	B
CA	Folsom Christmas Art and Craft	20,000	Dec	724-26 Sutter Street	Folsom	CA	95630	916-941-6714	B
CA	Peddlers Fair	30,000	Sep	724-26 Sutter Street	Folsom	CA	95630	530-241-4063	B
CA	Fine Art Show at River Park	40,000	Oct	1756 West Bullard	Fresno	CA	93650	559-449-9818	B
CA	Gilroy Garlic Festival	125,000	July	P O Box 2311	Gilroy	CA	95021	408-842-1625	B
CA	Indio Tamale Festival	120,000	Dec	100 Civic Center Mall	Indio	CA	92201	760-342-6532	B
CA	Fiesta Broadway	55,000	Apr	2130 San Telle Blvd Ste 304	Los Angeles	CA	90025	310-914-1933	B

CA	Spring May Day Fair	55,000	Apr	P. O. Box 71	Los Banos	CA	93635	209-826-5166	B
CA	California Peach Festival	62,000	July	P. O. Box 3231	Marysville	CA	95993	530-671-9599	B
CA	Millbrae Art and Wine Festival	80,000	Aug	50 Victoria Ave. Ste. 103	Millbrae	CA	94030	415-697-8737	B
CA	Morro Bay Harbor Festival	25,000	Oct	P. O. Box 18696	Morro Bay	CA	93443	805-772-1155	B
CA	Four Seasons Arts & Crafts Fest	12,000	July	P. O. Box 5672	Norco	CA	92860	909-735-4751	B
CA	Great Dickens Christmas Fair	20,000	Nov	P. O. Box 1768	Novato	CA	94948	800-510-1558	B
CA	Southwest Arts Festival		Feb	P. O. Box 62	Palm Desert	CA	92261	760-346-0042	B
CA	Route 66 Rendez-vous	550,000	Sep	201 North 3. Street Ste 103	San Bernadino	CA	92401	800-867-8366	B
CA	San Carlos Art and Wine Faire	70,000	Oct	P. O. Box 1086	San Carlos	CA	94070	209-296-1195	B
CA	Castro Street Fair	150,000	Oct	P. O. Box 14405	San Francisco	CA	94114	415-841-1824	B
CA	San Francisco State A and C Fair	26,000	Apr	Sc T-115, 1650 Holloway	San Francisco	CA	94132	415-338-2444	B
CA	Almaden Valley Art and Wine	23,000	Sep	P. O. Box 20084	San Jose	CA	95160		B
CA	Berryessa Art and Wine Festival	7,000	May	1127 Summer garden Ct.	San Jose	CA	95132	408-272-1578	B
CA	Artwalk Festival of Art	5,000	Oct	2559 Puesta Del Sol	Santa Barbara	CA	93105	805-682-4711	B

CA	Sherman Oaks Street Fair	80,000	Oct	14827 Ventura Blvd. Ste 207	Sherman Oaks	CA	91403	818-906-1951	B
CA	Asparagus Festival	100,000	Apr	425 N. El Dorado St.	Stockton	CA	95202	209-937-7488	B
CA	Tehachapi Mountain Festival	40,000	Aug	P. O. Box 401	Tehachapi	CA	93561	661-822-4180	B
CA	Redwood Empire Fair	25,000	Aug	1055 North State Street	Ukiah	CA	95482	707-462-3884	B
CA	Fairfield Candy Festival	50,000	Oct	1000 Texas Street #D	Fairfield	CA	94533	707-422-0103	B
CA	Country Folk Art Craft Show	20,000	Nov	15045 Dixie Highway	Holly	MI	48442	248-634-4151	B
CA	Topanga Country Fair	12,000	May	P. O. Box 1611	Topanga	CA	90290	310-455-1890	B
CO	Vail Arts Festival	20,000	July	P O Box 1153	Vail	CO	81658	970-476-4255	A
CO	Colorado Springs Territory Days	140,000	May	211 Farragut	Colorado Springs	CO	80909	719-475-0955	A-
CO	A Taste Of Colorado	500,000	Sep	511 16th St. Ste 200	Denver	CO	80202	303-295-6330	A-
CO	Snowmass Arts And Crafts Fair	10,000	July	P. O. Box 5566	Snow-mass Village	CO	81615	970-923-2000	A-
CO	Cherry Creek Arts Festival	350,000	July	2 Steele Street B100	Denver	CO	80206	303-355-2787	A+
CO	Downtown Boulder Fall Festival	55,000	Sep	1942 Broad-way #301	Boulder	CO	80302	303-484-0820	B
CO	Artfair	50,000	July	P. O. Box 1634	Boulder	CO	80306	303-499-0199	B

CO	Brecken-ridge July Art Festival	30,000	July	P. O. Box 2938	Breckenridge	CO	80424	970-547-9326	B
CO	Mountain Fair	15,000	July	P O Box 175	Carbon-dale	CO	81623	970-963-1680	B
CO	Capitol Hill Peoples Fair	275,000	Jun	1490 Lafayette #104	Denver	CO	80218	303-830-1651	B
CO	Greely Arts Picnic	33,000	July	651 Tenth Avenue	Greeley	CO	80631	970-350-9451	B
CO	Manitou Springs A and C Fest.	30,000	Sep	P. O. Box 42	Manitou Springs	CO	80829	719-577-7700	B
CO	Beaver Creek Arts Festival	25,000	Aug	9695 West Broward	Plantation	FL	33324	954-472-3755	B
CO	Denver's Holiday Gift Festival	33,000	July	P. O. Box 91369	Portland	OR	97291	503-526-1080	B
CO	Steamboat Springs Art In The Park	10,000	July	P. O. Box 774284	Steam-boat Springs	CO	80477	970-879-9008	B
CT	Westport Handcrafts Show	10,000	May	10 Lyons Plains Road	Weston	CT	06883	203-227-7844	A
CT	Oyster Festival	90,000	Sep	132 Water St.	South Norwalk	CT	06854	203-838-9444	A-
CT	Creative Arts Festival	8,000	Nov	144 limperial Ave.	Westport	CT	06880	203-222-1388	A-
CT	Guilford Handcraft Exhib.	20,000	July	P. O. Box 589	Gilford	CT	06437	203-453-5947	A+
CT	Craft Village Arts And Crafts Festival	10,000	Oct	779 East Main St.	Branford	CT	06405	203-488-4689	B
CT	On The Green Art And Craft Show	10,000	Sep	P. O. Box 304	Glaston-bury	CT	06033	203-659-1196	B
CT	Mystic Seaport Outdoor Art	60,000	Aug	P. O. Box 300	Mystic	CT	06355	860-572-7844	B

CT	Christmas Crafts Expo	18,000	Dec	P. O. Box 227	North Granby	CT	06060	860-653-6671	B
CT	Old Saybrook Art & Craft	250,000	July	P. O. Box 625	Old Saybrook	CT	06475	860-388-3266	B
CT	Sono Arts Celebration	60,000	Aug	P O Box 500	South Norwalk	CT	06856	203-866-7916	B
CT	Downtown Merchants Outdoor Art Show	30,000	July	P O Box 5132	Westport	CT	06880	203-454-8688	B
CT	Celebrate West Hardford A & C Show	30,000	May	50 South Main Street	West Hartford	CT	06107	860-570-3705	B
DC	Washington Craft Show	10,000	Nov	P. O. Box 603	Greens Farms	CT	06436	203-254-0486	A+
DC	Smithsonian Craft Show	20,000	Apr	A & I Bldg, Rm 1465	Washing-ton	DC	20560	202-357-4000	A+
DC	National Christmas Show	38,000	Nov	P. O. Box 11565	Winston Salem	NC	27116	910-924-8337	A+
DE	Brandywine Arts Festival	35,000	Sep	2903 B Philadelp hia Pike	Wilming-ton	DE	19703	302-529-0761	A-
DE	Deleware Fine Art And Craft Show	10,000	Jul	P. O. Box 347	Ardmore	PA	19003	877-244-9768	B
DE	Dover Offi. Spouses Club Craft Show	10,000	Nov	P. O. Box 02069	Dover	DE	19901	302-677-6032	B
DE	Sea Witch Halloween And Fiddlers	150,000	Oct	P. O. Box 216	Rehoboth Beach	DE	19971	302-227-2233	B
FL	Festival Of The Masters	125,000	Nov	Box 10150 (Walt Disney	Lake Buena Vista	FL	32830	407-934-6743	A
FL	Fiesta In The Park	200,000	Nov	P. O. Box 1883	Orlando	FL	32802	407-246-2827	A

FL	Old Hyde Park Village Art Festival	65,000	Oct	9695 West Broward Blvd	Plantation	FL	33324	954-472-3755	A
FL	Market Days	16,000	Dec	3491 11 Thomas Road	Tallahas-see	FL	32308	850-576-9820	A
FL	Gasparilla Festival Of The Arts	300,000	Mar	P O Box 10591	Tampa	FL	33679	813-876-1747	A
FL	Isle Of Eight Flags Shrimp Fest	175,000	May	P.O. Box 1251	Fernand-ina Beach	FL	32035	904-261-7020	A-
FL	Holiday Arts And Crafts Show	12,000	Nov	Pmb 275, 16520 Tamiami Trail #18	Fort Meyers	FL	33908	508-737-0998	A-
FL	Riverwalk Arts And Crafts Show	100,000	Jan.	301 N. Andrews Ave	Ft. Lauder-dale	FL	33301	305-761-5359	A-
FL	Mount Dora Craft Show	250,000	Oct	P. O. Box 378	Mount Dora	FL	32756	352-735-1191	A-
FL	Artigras Fine Arts Festival	150,000	Feb	3970 RCA Blvd. Ste 7010	Palm Beach Gardens	FL	33410	561-691-8506	A-
FL	Great Gulfcoast Art Festival	150,000	Nov	P. O. Box 10744	Pensacola	FL	32524	904-432-9906	A-
FL	Baptist Hospital Artist's Showcase	30,000	Apr	P. O. Box 800035	Roswell	GA	30075	800-293-4983	A-
FL	Mainsail Arts Festival	90,000	Apr	P O Box 2842	St. Peters-burg	FL	33731	727-892-5885	A-
FL	Sunfest	325,000	May	525 Clematis St.	West Palm Beach	FL	33401	561-659-5980	A-
FL	Winter Park Autumn Art Festival	60,000	Oct	P. O. Box 280	Winter Park	FL	32790	407-646-2284	A-
FL	Boca Museum Art Festival	50,000	Feb	801 W. Palmetto Park Rd.	Boca Raton	FL	33486	561-392-2500	A+

FL	Coconut Grove Arts Festival	800,000	Feb	3427 Main Highway	Coconut Grove	FL	33233	305-447-0401	A+
FL	Old Island Days Art Festival	25,000	Feb	3124 Riviera Dr.	Key West	FL	3040	305-294-0431	A+
FL	Christmas Made In The South	35,000	Nov	P. O. Box 853	Matthews	NC	28106	704-847-9480	A+
FL	Florida Strawberry Festival	600,000	Feb	P. O. Drawer 1869	Plant City	FL	33564	813-752-9194	A+
FL	Winter Park Sidewalk Art Festival	350,000	Mar	P. O. Box 597	Winter Park	FL	32789	407-672-6390	A+
FL	Fall Country Jamboree	18,000	Nov	P. O. Box 5	Barberville	FL	32105	386-749-2959	B
FL	Arts Festival	150,000	Mar	1800 N. Dixie Hwy.	Boca Raton	FL	33432	407-395-4433	B
FL	Fiesta Of Arts	30,000	Feb	150 Nw Crawford Blvd	Boca Raton	FL	33432	407-393-7827	B
FL	The Riverview Art Fest.	10,000	Jan.	P. O. Box 1346	Cape Coral	FL	33910	941-945-1988	B
FL	Celebration Fall Art Festival	50,000	Oct	671 Front Street Ste 210	Celebra-tion	FL	34747	407-566-1200	B
FL	Art Harvest in the Park	60,000	Nov	1265 Bayshor e Blvd.	Clear-water	FL	34698	727-738-5523	B
FL	Space Coast Art Festival	100,000	Nov	P. O. Box 320135	Cocoa Beach	FL	32932	407-784-3322	B
FL	Banyan Arts & Crafts Festival	40,000	Nov	2820 Mcfarlan e Rd.	Coconut Grove	FL	33233	305-444-7270	B
FL	Florida Manatee Fine Arts	40,000	Feb	28 Nw Hwy 19	Crystal River	FL	34428	904-795-3149	B
FL	Deerfield Beach Fest. Of The Arts	25,000	Jan.	150 N.E. 2nd Ave	Deerfield Beach	FL	33441	454-421-6161	B

FL	Deland Fall Festival Of The Arts	54,000	Nov	P. O. Box 3194	Deland	FL	32721	386-738-5705	B
FL	Delray Affair	250,000	Apr	64 Se 5th Ave.	Delray Beach	FL	33483	561-279-1380	B
FL	Lido Keys Holiday A And C Show	12,000	Dec	16520 S. Tamaimi Trail #18	Fort Myers	FL	33908	508-737-0998	B
FL	Fishermen's Village Fall A And C	16,000	Oct	16520 S. Tamaima Trail #18	Fort Myers	FL	33908	508-737-0998	B
FL	Naples Art And Craft Show	12,000	Mar	16520 S. Tamaimi Trail #18	Fort Myers	FL	33908	508-737-0998	B
FL	Saint Simon's On The Sound Craft	25,000	Nov	28 Miricle Strip Parkway	Fort Walton Beach	FL	32548	850-244-8621	B
FL	Promenade In The Park	75,000	Nov	P. O. Box 2307	Ft Lauder-dale	FL	33303	954-764-5973	B
FL	Santa Fe C. College Spring Arts Fest	129,000	Apr	3000 Nw 83rd St.	Gaines-ville	FL	32606	352-392-5355	B
FL	Carols In The Park	28,000	Dec	P. O. Box 2237	Haines City	FL	33845	239-573-6764	B
FL	Acc Craft Fair	11,000	Dec	21 South Eltings Corner R	Highland	NY	12528	800-836-3470	B
FL	Anna Maria Island Winterfest	20,000	Dec	5312 Holmes Blvd.	Holms Beach	FL	34217	941-778-2099	B
FL	Homosas-sa Art, Craft And Seafood	30,000	Nov	P. O. Box 709	Homosas-sa	FL	34447	352-628-2666	B
FL	Artworks	3,000	May	P O Box 41564	Jackson-ville	FL	32203	904-387-7007	B
FL	Heathrow Festival Of The Arts	125,000	Oct	P. O. Box 952125	Lake Mary	FL	32795	407-585-2086	B
FL	Lutz Arts And Crafts Festival	35,000	Dec	P. O. Box 656	Lutz	FL	33548	813-949-7060	B

FL	Grouper Fest And Art Market	24,000	Oct	150 John's Pass Boardwlk	Madeira Beach	FL	33706	813-645-4954	B
FL	1890's Mcintosh Festival	35,000	Oct	P. O. Box 1890	Mcintosh	FL	32664	352-591-1890	B
FL	Miami Beach Festival Of The Arts	50,000	Mar	1700 Civic Center Drive	Miami Beach	FL	33139	305-673-7577	B
FL	Mount Dora Arts Festival	250,000	Feb	138 E 5th Ave	Mount Dora	FL	32757	352-383-0880	B
FL	Images In Art Show	30,000	Oct	P. O. Box 6229	Ocala	FL	34478	352-867-4788	B
FL	Halifax Art Festival	20,000	Oct	P. O. Box 2038	Ormond Beach	FL	32175	904-673-2098	B
FL	Great Day In The Country	60,000	Nov	P. O. Box 621607	Oviedo	FL	32762	407-365-9420	B
FL	Florida Azalea Festival	25,000	Mar	623 Saint Johns Ave.	Palatka	FL	32177	386-328-4021	B
FL	Palm Harbor Arts, Crafts And Music	15,000	Dec	1151 Nebras-ka Avenue	Palm Harbor	FL	34683	727-784-4287	B
FL	Saint Andrews Fall Seafood Fest	22,000	Sep	1618 Isabella Avenue	Panama City	FL	32410	850-784-9542	B
FL	Downtown Delray Festival	125,000	Jan.	9695 West Broward Blvd	Plantation	FL	33324	954-472-3755	B
FL	Los Olas Art Fair	100,000	Jan.	1350 W. Broward Blvd.	Plantation	FL	33324	954-472-3755	B
FL	Downtown Festival Of The Arts	90,000	Feb	9695 West Broward	Plantation	FL	33324	954-472-3755	B

FL	Plantation Art In The Park	50,000	Oct	P. O. Box 15473	Plantation	FL	33318	954-797-9762	B
FL	Safety Harbor Holiday Art	30,000	Dec	125 5th Ave. North	Safety Harbor	FL	34695	727-725-1562	B
FL	Saint Cloud Craft Festival	18,000	Dec	P. O. Box 700522	Saint Cloud	FL	34770	407-892-1667	B
FL	Rotary Club Arts And Crafts Fair	10,000	Feb	Box 736	Sanibel	FL	33957	239-489-4862	B
FL	Museum Of Art Las Olas Art Festival	50,000	Mar	8 Seneca Road	Sea Ranch Lakes	FL	33308	954-942-9697	B
FL	Highlands Art Festival	20,000	Nov	351 W. Center Avenue	Sebring	FL	33870	863-385-5312	B
FL	Artexpo South Miami	45,000	Jan	7800 Red Road, Ste 215d	South Miami	FL	33143	305-558-1758	B
FL	Beaux Arts Festival Of Art	100,000	Jan.	P O Box 431216	South Miami	FL	33143	305-789-9254	B
FL	South Miami Art Festival	60,000	Nov	6410 Sw 80th	South Miami	FL	33143	305-661-1621	B
FL	St Augustine Art & Crafts Festival	25,000	Mar	22 Marine St	St. Aug-ustine	FL	32084	904-824-0716	B
FL	Temple Terrace Comm. Arts	15,000	Nov	P. O. Box 291266	Temple Terrace	FL	33687	813-989-7181	B
FL	Indian River Festival A And C Show	30,000	Apr	2000 S. Washington St. 1	Titusville	FL	32780	321-267-3036	B
GA	Dogwood Festival	300,000	Apr	20 Exec. Park Dr # 2019	Atlanta	GA	30329	404-329-0501	A
GA	Prater's Mill Country Fair	10,000	May	848 Sugart Rd	Dalton	GA	30720	706-275-6455	A
GA	Mossy Creek Barnyard A And C	20,000	Oct	106 Anne Drive	Warner Robins	GA	31093	912-922-8265	A

GA	Cotton Pickin' Country Fair	30,000	Oct	P. O. Box 1	Gay	GA	30218	706-538-6814	A-
GA	Brown's Crossing Festival	12,000	Oct	400 Brown's Crossing	Milledge-ville	GA	31061	912-452-9327	A-
GA	Peachtree Crossings County Fair	30,000	Sep	3869 Redbud Court	Smyrna	GA	30082	404-434-3661	A-
GA	Arts Festival Of Atlanta	100,000	Sep	140 First Union	Atlanta,	GA	30309	404-589-8777	A+
GA	Peachtree Art And Craft Show	13,000	Nov	4664 N. Peach-tree Rd.	Dunwoody	GA	30338	404-451-4613	A+
GA	Georgia Mountain Fair	100,000	Aug	P. O. Box 444 Us 76 W	Hiawas-see	GA	30546	706-896-4191	A+
GA	Powers' Crossroads Art Fest	50,000	Aug	4766 W. Hwy. 34	Newnan	GA	30263	770-253-2011	A+
GA	Yellow Daisy Festival	200,000	Sep	P. O. Box 778	Stone Mountain	GA	30086	770-498-5633	A+
GA	Canton Riverfest	24,000	Sep	P. O. Box 1132	Canton	GA	30169	770-704-5991	B
GA	Paulding Meadows A And C Festival	25,000	Sep	P. O. Box 654	Dallas	GA	30132	770-505-1987	B
GA	Possum Hollow Arts And Crafts Fair	15,000	Sep	P. O. Box 584	Dexter	GA	31019	478-875-3200	B
GA	Duluth Fall Festival	95,000	Sep	P. O. Box 497	Duluth	GA	30096	770-476-0240	B
GA	Mule Camp Market	50,000	Oct	P. O. Box 36	Gaines-ville	GA	30503	770-714-9309	B
GA	Lazy Daze In Georgia, Georgia Mall	50,000	Jul	5010 Strick-land Rd	Gainse-ville	GA	30507	770-967-4753	B
GA	Calico Holiday Arts And Crafts	15,000	Nov	290-G Harper Blvd.	Moultrie	GA	31788	229-985-1968	B

GA	Norcross Artfest	15,000	Oct	P. O. Box 331	Norcross	GA	30091	770-729-0200	B
GA	Million Pines A And C Festival	15,000	Nov	P. O. Box 135	Soperton	GA		912-529-6611	B
IA	Autumn Fest Arts & Crafts Affair	20,000	Oct	Box 184	Boys Town	NE	68010	402-331-2889	A
IA	Art In The Park	5,000	Jun	P. O. Box 2164	Clinton,	IA	52733	815-772-8856	B
IA	Quad Cty Riverssance Fine Arts	15,000	Sep	P. O. Box 2183	Davenport	IA	52809	319-386-7013	B
IA	Beaux Art Invitational Spring Fair	27,000	May	3 North Garfield Ct.	Davenport	IA	52801	563-323-9042	B
IA	Two Rivers Art Expo.	8,000	Nov	4055 Sw 30th St.	Des Moines	IA	50321	515-285-6765	B
IA	Iowa Arts Festival	40,000	Jun	P. O. Box 3128	Iowa City	IA	52244	319-337-7944	B
IA	Storm Lake Spectac-ular	30,000	Jul	P. O. Box 584	Storm Lake	IA	50588	712-732-3787	B
ID	Sun Valley Arts & Crafts Festival	20,000	Aug	P. O. Box 656	Ketchum	ID	83353	208-726-9491	A+
ID	Boise River Festival	500,000	Jun	404 S. 8th St. Ste 404	Boise	ID	83702	208-338-8887	B
ID	Art In The Park	175,000	Sep	670 S Julia Davis Dr.	Boise	ID	83702	208-345-8330	B
ID	Mccall Winter Carnival	75,000	Jan	P. O. Box 350	Mccall	ID	83638	208-634-7631	B
IL	Greenwich Village Art Fair	15,000	Sep	711 N. Main St.	Rockford	IL	61103	815-968-2787	A
IL	Holiday Folk Craft And Art	25,000	Nov	P. O. Box 228	Rockton	IL	61072	815-629-2060	A
IL	Art On The Square	42,000	May	P. O. Box 23561	Belleville	IL	62223	618-257-0747	A-

IL	North Halstead Mkt. Days	200,000	Sep	1960 N. Clybourn R Bldg.	Chicago	IL	60614	773-868-3010	A-
IL	Autumn Festival	30,000	Nov	P. O. Box 184	Boys Town	NE	68010	402-331-2889	A+
IL	Celebrate On State Street	600,000	Jun	16w129 83rd Street	Burr Ridge	IL	60521	708-325-8080	A+
IL	Old Town Art Fair	40,000	Jun	1763 North Park Ave	Chicago	IL	60614	312-337-1938	A+
IL	57th Street Art Fair	100,000	Jun	1763 North Park Ave	Chicago	IL	60614	312-337-1938	A+
IL	American Craft Exposition	13,000	Aug	Henry Crown Sports Pavilion	Evanston	IL	60201	708-570-5099	A+
IL	Port Clinton Art Festival	275,000	Aug	90 Oak-wood, Ste 101	Lincoln-shire	IL	60069	847-444-9600	A+
IL	Invitational Crafts Exhibit	100,000	Jul	P O Box 1350	Oak Brook	IL	60522	630-573-0700	A+
IL	Midwest Craft Festival	40,000	May	620 Lincoln Avenue	Winnetka	IL	60093	708-446-2870	A+
IL	Old Orchard Craft Festival	100,000	May	620 Lincoln Avenue	Winnetka	IL	60093	708-446-2870	A+
IL	Arlington Race-course Art And Folk	15,000	Nov	16W129 83rd Street	Burr Ridge	IL	60521	630-325-8080	B
IL	Lambs Farm Holiday Art And Craft	20,000	Dec	16W129 83rd Street	Burr Ridge	IL	60521	630-325-8080	B
IL	Orland Square Art And Craft Show	50,000	Feb	16W129 83rd Street	Burr Ridge	IL	60521	630-325-8080	B
IL	Carlinville Christmas Market	15,000	Dec	126 Main Street	Carlinville	IL	62626	217-854-2141	B
IL	Urbana Arts And Crafts Festival	50,000	Jun	301 North Randolf	Cham-paign	IL	61820	217-398-2376	B

IL	Chicago's New E. Side Artworks	70,000	Aug	857 W. Webster Ave	Chicago	IL	60614	773-404-0763	B
IL	Brookfest Summer Festival	20,000	Jul	1960 N. Clybourn R Bldg.	Chicago	IL	60614	773-868-3010	B
IL	Evanston Lakeshore Arts Fest.	20,000	Aug	927 Noyes	Evanston	IL	60201	847-448-8260	B
IL	Evanston Ethnic Arts Festival	20,000	Jul	927 Noyes Street	Evanston	IL	60201	847-448-8260	B
IL	Midwest Salute To The Masters	40,000	Aug	P. O. Box 2032	Fairview Heights	IL	62208	618-394-0022	B
IL	Galena Arts Festival	6,000	Jul	P. O. Box 23	Galena	IL	61036	815-777-9341	B
IL	Hinsdale Fine Arts Festival	5,000	Jun	22 E First St	Hinsdale	IL	60521	708-323-3952	B
IL	Lagrange West End Art Festival	30,000	Sep	106 Calendar Ave.	Lagrange	IL	60525	630-536-8416	B
IL	Cedarhurst Craft Fair	20,000	Sep	P. O. Box 923 Richview Rd	Mt Vernon	IL	62864	618-242-1236	B
IL	Riverwalk Art Fair	20,000	Sep	508 N Center	Naperville	IL	60563	708-355-2530	B
IL	Water Tower Arts & Craft Fest.	25,000	Jun	P. O. Box 1326	Palatine,	IL	60078	312-751-2500	B
IL	Fine Art Fair	40,000	Sep	203 Harrison	Peoria	IL	61602	309-637-2787	B
IL	Springfield Old Capitol Art Fair	25,000	May	1508 Daylilly Pl	Springfield	IL	62707	217-585-8000	B
IN	4th St. Festival Of The Arts & Crafts	25,000	Aug	P O Box 1257	Blooming-ton	IN	47402	812-334-4447	A-
IN	Chesterton Arts & Crafts Fair	10,000	Aug	P. O. Box 783	Chester-ton	IN	46304	219-926-4711	A-

IN	Leeper Park Art Fair	10,000	Jun	16200 Continen tal Drive	Granger	IN	46530	574-272-8598	A-
IN	Covered Bridge Festival	750,000	Oct	7975 E. Chandler Avenue	Terre Haute	IN	47803	812-877-9550	A-
IN	Covered Bridge Festival	900,000	Oct	7975 E. Chandler Ave.	Terre Haute	IN	47803	812-877-9550	A-
IN	Amish Acres Arts And Crafts	80,000	Aug	1600 W. Market Street	Nappanee	IN	46550	574-773-4188	A+
IN	Chautau-qua Of The Arts	25,000	Sep	P. O. Box 2624	Columbus	IN	47202	812-265-5080	B
IN	Talbot Street Art Fair	60,000	Jun	P. O. Box 44166	Danville	IN	46244	317-745-6479	B
IN	Talbot Street Art Fair	60,000	Jun	Box 489	Danville,	IN	46122	317-887-9853	B
IN	Broad Ripple Art Fair	20,000	May	820 E 67th St.	Indianap-olis	IN	46220	317-255-2464	B
IN	Round The Fountain Art Fair	5,000	May	P O Box 1134	Lafayette	IN	47902	317-477-4230	B
IN	Chautau-qua Festival Of Art	75,000	Sep	601 West First St.	Madison	IN	47250	812-265-6100	B
KS	Arts And Crafts Fair	40,000	Sep	109 South Main	Hillsboro	KS	67063	620-947-3506	A-
KS	Overland Park Arts And Crafts Fair	15,000	Sep	6300 West 87th Street	Overland Park	KS	66212	913-895-6357	B
KS	Smoky Hill River Festival	100,000	Jun	P. O. Box 2181	Salina	KS	67402	913-823-1900	B
KS	Christmas In July	10,000	Jul	Box 12707	Wichita	KS	67212	316-773-9300	B
KS	Wichita Art And Book Fair	40,000	May	P. O. Box 20885	Wichita	KS	67208	316-683-3144	B

KS	Pioneer Christmas Arts And Crafts	12,000	Nov	P. O. Box 9024	Wichita	KS	67277	316-729-9443	B
KY	St. James Court Art Show	300,000	Oct	P. O. Box 3804	Louisville	KY	40201	502-635-1842	A
KY	St. James Ct. Art Fair Belgravia	300,000	Oct	511 Belgravia Ct.	Louisville	KY	40201	502-634-8950	A
KY	Louisville Christmas Show	13,000	Nov	P. O. Box 66	Madison	IN	47250	812-265-6100	A
KY	St. James Ct Art Show S. 4th Street	300,000	Oct	P. O. Box 186	Louisville	KY	40201	502-634-8587	A+
KY	Bardstown Arts, Crafts, And Antiques	12,000	Oct	P. O. Box 867	Bardstown	KY	40004	502-348-4877	B
KY	Holiday Fine Art And Craft Fair	8,000	Nov	P. O. Box 21882	Columbus	OH	43221	614-486-3537	B
KY	Cincinnati Winterfair	13,000	Nov	1665 West Fifth Ave	Columbus	KY	43212	614-486-7119	B
KY	Newport Arts And Music Festival	20,000	Jul	915 Lincoln Road	Dayton	KY	41074	859-441-3139	B
KY	Cherokee Triangle Art Fair	25,000	Apr	P. O. Box 4306	Louisville	KY	40204	502-458-3905	B
LA	Christmas In New Orleans	17,000	Nov	16471 Highway 40	Folsom	LA	70437	504-796-5853	A
LA	New Orleans Jazz & Heritage Festival	500,000	Apr	1205 North Rampart St.	New Orleans	LA	70116	504-522-4786	A-
LA	Covington Three Rivers Art Festival	35,000	Nov	P. O. Box 633	Covington	LA	70434	985-705-7968	B
LA	Kenner Christmas In Jul A And C	15,000	Jul	16741 Highway 40	Folsom	LA	70437	985-796-5853	B

LA	Red River Revel Arts Festival	200,000	Sep	101 Milam	Shreve-port	LA	71101	318-424-4000	B
MA	Christmas Festival	37,000	Nov	83 Mt. Vernon Street	Boston	MA	02108	617-742-3973	A
MA	Crafts At The Castle	10,000	Dec	34 1/2 Beacon St.	Boston	MA	02108	617-523-6400	A
MA	Old Deerfield Christmas Sampler	17,000	Nov	P. O. Box 323	Deerfield	MA	1342	413-774-7476	A-
MA	Danforth Craft Festival	5,000	Jun	123 Union Ave.	Framingh am	MA	01701	508-620-0050	A+
MA	Festival Of The Arts	10,000	Aug	154 Crowell Rd	Chatham	MA	02633	508-945-3583	B
MA	Original Castleberry	25,000	Nov	38 Charles Street	Rochester	NH	03867	603-332-2616	B
MD	National Craft Fair	25,000	Oct	4845 Rumler Rd	Chambers burg	PA	17201	717-369-4810	A
MD	Sunfest	200,000	Sep	200 125th Street	Ocean City	MD	21842	410-250-0125	A
MD	Sugarloaf Crafts Festival	26,000	Oct	200 Orchard Ridge Dr. #215	Gaithers-burg	MD	20878	800-210-9900	A
MD	Fell's Point Fun Festival	700,000	Oct	812 South Ann St.	Baltimore	MD	21231	410-675-6756	A-
MD	Acc Craft Fair	35,000	Mar	72 Spring St.	New York	NY	10012	212-274-0630	A+
MD	Fells Point Art & Craft Show	6,000	Aug	1606 Portugul St.	Baltimore	MD	21231	410-563-2606	B
MD	Artscape	750,000	Jul	7 E. Red-wood St. Ste 500	Baltimore	MD	21202	410-752-8632	B
MD	Bel Air Festival For The Arts	30,000	Sep	1909 Wheel Road	Bel Air	MD	21015	410-836-2395	B

MD	Waterfowl Festival	15,000	Nov	P. O. Box 929	Easton	MD	21601	410-822-4567	B
MD	Frederick Festival Of The Arts	25,000	Jun	P O Box 3080	Frederick	MD	21705	301-694-9632	B
MD	Sugarloaf Crafts Festival	24,000	Apr	200 Orchard Ridge Dr.#215	Gaithers-burg	MD	20878	800-210-9900	B
MD	Christmas Wonder-land	20,000	Nov	P. O. Box 1921	Hager-stown	MD	21742	301-791-2346	B
MD	Havre De Grace Arts And Crafts	10,000	Aug	P. O. Box 150	Havre De Grace	MD	21078	410-939-9342	B
MD	Shaker Forest Festival	37,000	Sep	275 Pleasant view Dr.	Midland	PA	15059	724-643-6627	B
MD	North Beach Bayfest	18,000	Aug	P. O. Box 99	North Beach	MD	20714	301-855-6681	B
MD	Ocean City Holiday Shoppers Fair	15,000	Nov	4001 Coastal Highway	Ocean City	MD	21842	410-289-8311	B
MD	Christmas Craft Expo.	10,000	Nov	10549 Sussex Rd.	Ocean City	MD	21842	410-524-9177	B
MD	Kennedy Krieger Festival Of Trees	25,000	Nov	200 E. Joppa Road #403	Towson	MD	21204	410-769-8223	B
MD	Towsontown Spring Festival	250,000	May	P O Box 10115	Towson	MD	21285	410-825-1144	B
MD	Brandy-wine Lions Craft Fair Festival	20,000	Oct	13200 Old Marlboro Pike	Upper Marlboro	MD	20772	301-627-7575	B
MD	Cabin Fever Festival		Feb	P. O. Box 187	Walkers-ville	MD	21793	301-898-5466	B
MD	Ocean City Labor Day A And C Fest.	15,000	Sep	9005 Whaley-ville Road	Whaley-ville	MD	21872	410-524-9177	B

ME	Bath Heritage Days	50,000	Jul	60 Pleasant Polnt Rd	Topsham	ME	04086	207-373-1325	B
MI	Allen Park Arts And Crafts	50,000	Aug	16850 Southfield Road	Allen Park	MI	48101	313-928-1400	A
MI	South Univ. Art Fair	100,000	Jul	P. O. Box 4525	Ann Arbor	MI	48106	734-663-5300	A
MI	Flint Art Fair	20,000	Jun	1120 E Kearsley St.	Flint	MI	48503	810-234-1695	A
MI	Chrysler Arts, Beats And Eats	800,000	Sep	17 Water St.	Pontiac	MI	48342	248-975-8812	A
MI	Birmingham Art In The Park	60,000	Sep	7 South Perry St	Pontiac	MI	48342	810-456-8150	A-
MI	The Ann Arbor Street Art Fair	500,000	Jul	P O Box 1352	Ann Arbor	MI	48106	734-994-5260	A+
MI	State Street Area Art Fair	500,000	Jul	P. O. Box 4128	Ann Arbor	MI	48106	313-663-6511	A+
MI	The Summer Art Fair	500,000	Jul	118 N. Fourth Ave.	Ann Arbor	MI	48104	313-662-3382	A+
MI	Art & Apples Festival	150,000	Sep	407 Pine St.	Rochester	MI	48307	810-651-7418	A+
MI	Royal Oak Outdoor Art Fair	30,000	Jul	P. O. Box 64	Royal Oak,	MI	48068	810-585-4736	A+
MI	Krasl Art Fair On The Bluff	75,000	Jul	707 Lake Blvd.	St. Joseph	MI	49085	616-983-0271	A+
MI	Algonac Rotary Art Fair	30,000	Sep	P. O. Box 1959	Algonac	MI	48001	810-794-5937	B
MI	Southfield City Art Fair	30,000	Aug	118 N. Fourth Ave	Ann Arbor	MI	48104	734-662-3382	B
MI	Summit Place Mall Show	80,000	Dec	40750 Woodward Ave32	Bloomfield Hills	MI	48304	248-302-1610	B
MI	Brighton Art Festival	20,000	Aug	131 Hyne Street	Brighton	MI	48116	810-227-5086	B

MI	Cadillac Festival Of The Arts	25,000	Jul	P. O. Box 841	Cadillac	MI	49601	231-775-7853	B
MI	Charlevoix Waterfront Art	30,000	Aug	Box 57	Charlevoix	MI	49720	616-547-5759	B
MI	Clarkston Art In The Village	15,000	Sep	P. O. Box 261	Clarkston	MI	48347	248-922-0270	B
MI	Clinton Fall Festival	60,000	Sep	P. O. Box 205	Clinton	MI	49236	517-456-7396	B
MI	Art On The Avenue	15,000	Jun	15801 Michigan Ave 4th	Dearborn	MI	48126	313-943-3095	B
MI	East Lansing Art Festival	50,000	May	410 Abbott Rd	East Lansing	MI	48823	517-319-6804	B
MI	MSU Crafts Fair	60,000	May	322 MSU Student Union	East Lansing	MI	48824	517-355-3354	B
MI	MSU Holiday Arts And Crafts	15,000	Dec	322 MSU Union	East Lansing	MI	48824	517-355-3354	B
MI	Shipshe-wana On the Road/Bat-tle Creek	10,000	Nov	10740 Three Mile Road	East Leroy	MI	49051	269-979-8888	B
MI	Farmington Founders Festival	65,000	Jul	P. O. Box 291	Farming-ton	MI	48332	248-932-3378	B
MI	Americana Folk Art Show	100,000	Sep	613 S. Main Street	Franken-muth	MI	48734	989-652-9701	B
MI	Hot Air Jubilee Arts And Crafts Show	60,000	Jul	3606 Wild-wood Avenue	Jackson	MI	49204	517-782-1515	B
MI	Lexington's Fine Art And Craft Street	20,000	Aug	7276 Huron Avenue	Lexington	MI	48450	810-359-5151	B
MI	Art On The Rocks	12,000	Jul	P. O. Box 9	Marquette	MI	49855	906-942-7865	B
MI	Cornwell's Sep Arts And Crafts	22,000	Sep	18935 15 1/2 Mile Road	Marshall	MI	49068	239-781-4293	B

MI	Petoskey Art In The Park	20,000	Jul	401 E. Mitchell St.	Petoskey	MI	49770	616-347-4150	B
MI	Art In The Park	75,000	Jul	51220 Northview	Plymouth	MI	48170	734-454-1314	B
MI	Saint Joseph Venetian Festival	120,000	Jul	P. O. Box 510	Saint Joseph	MI	49085	269-983-7917	B
MI	South Haven Art Fair	10,000	Jul	P. O. Box 505	South Haven	MI	49090	616-637-1041	B
MI	South Haven Summer Art	20,000	Jul	P. O. Box 505	South Haven	MI	49090	269-637-1041	B
MI	St Clair Art Fair	60,000	Jun	201 Riverside	St. Clair	MI	48079	810-329-9576	B
MI	Traverse Bay Fair	9,000	Jul	720 S. Elmwood	Traverse City	MI	49684	517-268-5656	B
MI	Saint Nick's Warehouse	11,000	Nov	P. O. Box 180359	Utica	MI	48318	586-566-1353	B
MI	Westland Summer Festival	225,000	Jul	7910 Nankin Mill Street	Westland	MI	48185	734-261-5955	B
MI	Wyandotte Heritage Days	40,000	Sep	2630 Biddle Avenue	Wyandotte	MI	48192	734-324-7297	B
MI	Art In The Park	230,000	Jul	587 West Western	Muskegon	MI	49440	231-722-6520	B
MN	Little Falls Sidewalk Arts And Crafts	65,000	Sep	200 Nw 1st Street	Little Falls	MN	56345	320-630-5155	A
MN	Minnesota Crafts Festival	15,000	Jun	528 Hennepin Ave. Ste 216	Minneapolis	MN	55403	612-333-7789	A
MN	Minnesota Renaissance Festival	312,000	Aug	3525 West 145th Street	Shakopee	MN	55379	612-445-7361	A

MN	Edina Art Fair	35,000	Jun	P. O. Box 24122	Edina	MN	55424	612-922-1524	A-
MN	Powderhorn Festival	60,000	Aug	P. O. Box 7372	Minneapolis	MN	55047	612-724-8179	A-
MN	Autumn Festival, An Arts & Crafts Affair	350,000	Nov	Box 184	Boys Town	NE	68010	402-331-2889	A+
MN	Metris Uptown Art Fair	300,000	Aug	1406 W. Lake St Ste 2002	Minneapolis	MN	55408	612-823-4581	A+
MN	Spring Festival An Arts & Crafts	12,000	Apr	Box 184	Boys Town	NE	68010	402-331-2889	B
MN	Maple Grove Days Art Fair	30,000	Jul	P. O. Box 2009	Maple Grove	MN	55311	612-494-5984	B
MN	River City Days	25,000	Aug	439 Main Street	Red Wing	MN	55066	651-388-4719	B
MN	Old Creamery Arts And Crafts Show	15,000	Sep	40 S. Main St. E Box 176	Rice	MN	56367	320-393-4100	B
MN	Highland Fest	65,000	Aug	790 Cleveland Ave S. #219	Saint Paul	MN	55116	651-699-9042	B
MN	Art At Ramsey Junior High	30,000	Dec	1015 South Snelling	Saint Paul	MN	55116	651-222-2483	B
MO	Plumb Nellie Festival And Craft Show	800,000	May	P. O. Box 1034	Branson	MO	65615	417-334-1548	A
MO	Laumeier Cont. Arts & Crafts Fair	20,000	May	12580 Rott	St. Louis	MO	63127	314-821-1209	A
MO	Autumn Daze Craft Show	800,000	Sep	P. O. Box 1034	Branson	MO	65615	417-334-1548	A-
MO	Plaza Arts Fair	270,000	Sep	310 Ward Parkway	Kansas City	MO	64112	816-753-0100	A+
MO	Brookside Art Annual	50,000	May	3920 W. 69th Terrace	Prarie Village	KS	66208	913-362-9668	A+

MO	Saint Louis Art Fair	100,000	Sep	7818 Forsyth Ste 210	St Louis	MO	63105	314-863-0278	A+
MO	Christmas Arts And Crafts Ext.	10,000	Nov	P. O. Box 901	Cape Girardeau	MO	63702	573-334-9233	B
MO	Central West End Art Fair And Taste	50,000	Jun	304-A North Euclud Ave.	Saint Louis	MO	63108	314-361-2850	B
MO	Historic Shaw Art Fair	15,000	Oct	2211 S. 39th St.	St Louis	MO	63110	314-771-3101	B
MS	Mississippi Fine Arts And Crafts	20,000	Oct	P. O. Box 347	Ardmore	PA	19003	877-244-9768	B
MS	Meridian Arts In The Park Fest.	17,000	Apr	P. O. Box 1405	Meridian	MS	39302	601-693-2787	B
MS	Oxford Double Decker Arts Fest.	50,000	Apr	107 Court-house Sq. Ste 1	Oxford	MS	38655	800-758-9177	B
MS	Picayune Fall Street Fair	55,000	Nov	P. O. Box 1656	Picayune	MS	39466	601-799-3070	B
MT	Summerfair	20,000	Jul	401 N. 27th St.	Billings	MT	59101	406-245-8688	A
MT	Bigfork Festival Of The Arts	14,000	Aug	P. O. Box 1892	Bigfork	MT	59911	406-881-4636	B
MT	Billings Strawberry Festival	15,000	Jun	2906 Third Ave N.	Billings	MT	59101	406-259-5454	B
MT	Arts In The Park	10,000	Jul	P. O. Box 83	Kalispell	MT	59901	406-755-5268	B
NC	Bele Chere	350,000	Jul	P. O. Box 7148	Asheville	NC	28802	828-259-5821	A
NC	Mountain Heritage Day	35,000	Sep	Wcu	Cullowhee	NC	28723	828-227-2169	A-
NC	Craftsmens Christmas Classic	35,000	Nov	1240 Oakland Ave	Greens-boro	NC	27403	336-274-5550	A-

NC	Cityfest Live	110,000	Apr	518 North Hwy 16	Denver	NC	28037	704-483-6266	A+
NC	Village Art And Craft Fair	20,000	Aug	7 Boston Way	Asheville	NC	28803	828-274-2831	B
NC	Sourwood Festival	30,000	Aug	201 East State Street	Black Mountain	NC	28711	828-669-2300	B
NC	Fine Arts And Crafts Showcase	15,000	Jul	P. O. Box 1229	Brevard	NC	28712	828-884-2787	B
NC	Centerfest	20,000	Oct	120 Morris Street	Durham	NC	27701	919-560-2722	B
NC	Holly Day Fair	20,000	Nov	2605 Fort Bragg Road	Fayette-ville	NC	28303	910-323-5509	B
NC	Craftsmens Classic	20,000	Apr	1240 Oakland Ave	Greens-boro	NC	27403	336-274-1084	B
NC	Craftscene & Market-place Fun 4th	100,000	Jul	P. O. Box 29212	Greens-boro	NC	27429	336-274-4595	B
NC	Seaboard Festival Day	25,000	Oct	P. O. Box 132	Hamlet	NC	28345	910-582-3505	B
NC	Carolina Designer Craftsmen Fair	10,000	Nov	P. O. Box 33791	Raleigh	NC	27636	919-571-4217	B
NC	Fourth Of July Festival	40,000	Jul	4841 Long Beach Road Se	Southport	NC	28461	910-457-6964	B
NC	Church Street Art And Craft	20,000	Oct	P. O. Box 1409	Waynes-ville	NC	28786	828-456-3517	B
NC	Ashe County Christmas In July	33,000	Jul	P. O. Box 1107	West Jefferson	NC	28694	336-246-5855	B
ND	Island Park Show	15,000	Aug	701 Main Aven	Fargo	ND	58103	701-476-6771	B

NE	Autumn Fest, An Arts & Crafts	30,000	Nov	Box 184	Boys Town	NE	68010	402-331-2889	A
NE	Omaha Summer Arts Fest.	80,000	Jun	P. O. Box 31036	Omaha	NE	68131	402-963-9020	A
NE	Country-side Village Art Fair	15,000	Jun	2336 S 138th	Omaha	NE	68144	402-333-9629	A-
NE	Art In The Park	16,000	Jul	Box 1368	Kearney	NE	68848	308-234-2662	B
NE	Rockbrook Village Art Fair	30,000	Sep	2800 S. 110 Ct. Ste 1	Omaha	NE	68144	402-390-0890	B
NH	Craftsmens Fair	50,000	Aug	205 North Main St.	Concord	NH	03301	603-224-3375	A+
NH	Mills Falls Autumn Craft Fest.	10,000	Oct	38 Charles Street	Rochester	NH	03867	603-332-2616	B
NH	New England Craft &Food	22,000	Nov	38 Charles Street	Rochester	NH	03867	603-332-2616	B
NH	Christmas Craft Show	9,000	Dec	38 Charles Street	Rochester	NH	03867	603-332-2616	B
NJ	Atlantic City Arts Alive	140,000	Aug	47 N. Tallahassee Ave	Atlantic City	NJ	08401	609-345-0899	A
NJ	Westfield Craft Market	10,000	Nov	P. O. Box 480	Slate Hill	NY	10973	914-355-2400	A
NJ	Art And Craft Show	30,000	Aug	P. O. Box 274	Stone Harbor	NJ	08247	609-368-4112	A-
NJ	Montclair Craft Show	5,000	Dec	P. O. Box 8252	Glen Ridge	NJ	7028	973-743-4110	A+
NJ	Morristown Craft Market	5,000	Oct	P. O. Box 2305	Morris-town	NJ	07062	201-263-8332	A+
NJ	Borden-town Cranberry Fest	40,000	Oct	P. O. Box 686	Bordentown	NJ	08505	609-499-4410	B
NJ	Chester Fall Craft Show	12,000	Sep	P. O. Box 330	Chester	NJ	07930	973-377-3260	B

NJ	Hadden-field Art And Craft	130,000	Jul	114 Kings Hiway E	Haddon-field	NJ	08033	856-216-7253	B
NJ	Fine Art And Crafts Show	16,000	Oct	12 Galaxy Court	Hillsbor-ough	NJ	08844	908-874-5247	B
NJ	Country Folk Art Craft Show	25,000	Oct	15045 Dixie Highway	Holly	MI	48442	248-634-4151	B
NJ	Peters Valley Craft Fair	10,000	Sep	19 Kuhn Rd	Layton	NJ	07851	973-948-5200	B
NJ	Spring Chester Craft Show	12,000	Jun	P. O. Box 613	Madison	NJ	07940	973-377-3260	B
NJ	Flemington Crafts Festival	30,000	Apr	Box 326	Masonville	NY	13804	607-265-3230	B
NJ	Little Falls Street Fair	15,000	Sep	5 Jeanette Lane	Milford	NJ	08848	908-996-3866	B
NM	Southwest Arts Festival	30,000	Nov	525 San Pedro NE., #107	Albuquer-que	NM	87108	505-262-2448	A
NM	Weems Artfest	50,000	Nov	2801-M Eubank Ne	Albuquer-que	NM	87112	505-293-6133	A
NM	Int. Balloon Fiesta	850,000	Oct	4401 Alameda N. E.	Albuquer-que	NM	87113	505-821-1000	B
NM	Wine Festival At Bernallo	18,000	Sep	P. O. Box 57060	Albuquer-que	NM	87187	505-867-3311	B
NM	Cloudcroft OctFest	3,000	Jul	P O Box 1290	Cloudcroft	NM	88317	505-682-2733	B
NM	Farmington Riverfest Fine Arts Fair	13,000	May	901 Fairgrou nds Rd.	Farming-ton	NM	87401	505-599-1140	B
NM	Santa Fe Fiesta Arts & Crafts Fair	30,000	Sep	P. O. Box 22303	Santa Fe	NM	87502	505-988-2889	B
NV	Best In The West Cook-Off	350,000	Sep	4790 Caughlin Parkway 507	Reno	NV	89509	775-324-6435	A-

NV	Reno Street Vibrations	40,000	Sep	4790 Caughlin Parkway 507	Reno	NV	89509	775-324-6435	B
NY	Fairport Canal Days	200,000	Jul	6 N. Main Street	Fairport	NY	14450	585-234-4323	A
NY	Quaker Arts Fest	90,000	Sep	P. O. Box 202	Orchard Park	NY	14127	716-655-4147	A
NY	West-hampton Outdoor Art Show	10,000	Aug	P. O. Box 1228	West-hampton Beach	NY	11978	516-288-3337	A
NY	Handmade In The Usa	12,000	Jan.	10 Bank Street #1200	White Plains	NY	10606	914-421-3287	A
NY	Allentown Art Festival	500,000	Jun	Ellicott Stn P.O. Bx 1566	Buffalo	NY	14205	716-881-4269	A
NY	Adirondack Mountain Craft Fair	12,000	Sep	P. O. Box 300	Charlotte	VT	05445	802-425-3399	A-
NY	Naples Grape Festival	100,000	Sep	P. O. Box 70	Naples	NY	14512	585-374-2240	A-
NY	Autumn Crafts On Columbus	50,000	Oct	461 Central Park West #1	New York	NY	10025	212-866-2239	A-
NY	Letchworth A And C Show And Sale	100,000	Oct	P. O. Box 249	Perry	NY	14530	585-237-3517	A-
NY	Corn Hill Arts Fest.	250,000	Jul	133 S. Fitzhugh	Rochester	NY	14608	585-262-3142	A-
NY	The Syracuse Arts & Crafts Festival	60,000	Jun	109 S. Warren St. Ste !900	Syracuse	NY	13202	315-422-8284	A-
NY	Amer. Crafts Fest. / Lincoln Center	100,000	Jun	P. O. Box 650	Montclair	NJ	07042	973-746-0091	A+
NY	Christmas In The Country	53,000	Nov	4310 Tilson Road	Wilming-ton	NC	28412	910-799-9424	A+

NY	Crafts Park Avenue	10,000	Apr	4 Deming St	Wood-stock	NY	12498	914-679-7277	A+
NY	Armonk Outdoor Art Show	14,000	Oct	One Boulder Trail	Armonk,	NY	10504	914-273-5986	B
NY	Albany Holiday Art And Craft Showcase	14,000	Dec	P. O. Box 404	Delmar	NY	12054	518-439-8379	B
NY	Ellicottville Fall Festival	40,000	Oct	P. O. Box 456	Ellicottville	NY	14731	716-699-5046	B
NY	Elms Christmas Craft Show	18,000	Nov	341 Spier Falls Rd	Greenfield Center	NY	12833	518-893-7488	B
NY	Haverstraw Street Festival	20,000	Sep	P. O. Box 159	Haver-straw	NY	10927	845-947-5646	B
NY	Maple Festival	40,000	Apr	2861 Clarks Corners Road	Marathon	NY	13803	607-849-3518	B
NY	Holiday Art And Craft Spectacu-lar	20,000	Dec	Box 326	Masonville	NY	13804	607-265-3230	B
NY	Craft Festivals	5,000	Jul	P O Box 89	Mayville	NY	14757	716 - 753-0240	B
NY	Washington Sq. Outdoor Art Exhibit	200,000	Aug	115 E 9th St. #7c	New York	NY	10003	212-982-6255	B
NY	Waterfront Art Festival	15,000	Jul	50 State Street	Pittsford	NY	14534	585-383-1472	B
NY	Crafts At Rhinebeck	15,000	Oct	P. O. Box 389	Rhinebeck	NY	12572	914-876-4001	B
NY	Park Avenue Arts Festival	25,000	May	171 Reser-voir Ave	Rochester	NY	14620	585-256-4960	B
NY	Clothesline Festival		Sep	500 Univer-sity Ave.	Rochester	NY	14607	585-473-7720	B
NY	Masapequa Park Street Fair	50,000	Aug	P. O. Box 477	Smithtown	NY	11787	631-724-5966	B

NY	West Hempstead Street Fair	20,000	Oct	P. O. Box 477	Smithtown	NY	11787	631-724-5966	B
NY	Market Street: A Festival Of Art	40,000	Jul	320 Mont-gomery St	Syracuse	NY	13202	315-472-4245	B
NY	Woodstock-New Paltz A & C Fair	25,000	Sep	P. O. Box 825	Wood-stock	NY	12498	845-679-8087	B
OH	Wonderful World Of Ohio Mart	20,000	Oct	714 Portage Path	Akron	OH	44303	216-836-5535	A
OH	Christkindl Market	10,000	Nov	1001 Market Ave. N.	Canton	OH	44702	216-453-7666	A
OH	Winterfair	19,000	Dec	1665 W. 5th	Columbus	OH	43212	614-486-7119	A
OH	Art On The Commons	15,000	Aug	2655 Olson Drive	Kettering	OH	45420	513-296-0294	A
OH	Boston Mills Artfest	25,000	Jun	P O Box 175	Peninsula	OH	44264	216-657-2334	A
OH	Art By The Falls	25,000	Jun	155 Bell St	Chagrin Falls	OH	44022	216-247-7507	A-
OH	Nutcracker Sweets	5,000	Oct	7743 Salem Drive	Hudson	OH	44236	216-650-4327	A-
OH	Visions Of Sugar-plums	10,000	Nov	P. O. Box 21093	S. Euclid	OH	44121	216-932-2603	A-
OH	Troy Strawberry Festival	175,000	Jun	405 S. W. Public Sq. #330	Troy	OH	45373	937-339-7714	A-
OH	Upper Arlington Labor Day Arts	30,000	Sep	3600 Tremont Rd.	Upper Arlington	OH	43221	614-583-5310	A-
OH	Westerville Music And Arts Fest.	40,000	Jul	99 Com-merce Park Dr.	Wester-ville	OH	43082	614-882-8917	A-
OH	The Christmas Show	60,000	Nov	P. O. Box 45395	Westlake	OH	44145	440-835-9627	A-

OH	Christmas In The Colonies	25,000	Nov	P. O. Box 40298	Bay Village	OH	44264	216-835-1765	A+
OH	Fine Craft Festival	7,000	Apr	26001 S Woodland	Beach-wood	OH	44122	216-831-0700	A+
OH	Cain Park Arts Festival	60,000	Jul	40 Severance Circle	Cleveland Heights	OH	44118	216-2913669	A+
OH	Columbus Arts Festival	500,000	Jun	100 E. Broad Street Ste 2250	Columbus	OH	43215	614-224-2606	A+
OH	Yankee Peddler Festival	100,000	Sep	171 Granger Rd. #159	Medina	OH	44256	330-665-3669	A+
OH	Shaker Woods Festival	100,000	Aug	46000 New England Square	New Waterford	OH	44445	216-457-7615	A+
OH	Salt Fork Arts & Crafts Fest.	50,000	Aug	7570 Marysville Road	Byesville	OH	43723	740-685-1350	B
OH	Clifton Arts And Musicfest	40,000	Jun	11650 Detroit Avenue	Cleveland	OH	44102	216-228-4383	B
OH	Craftfair At Hathaway Brown	11,000	Jun	1665 West 5th Avenue	Columbus	OH	43212	614-486-7119	B
OH	Kettering Holiday And Home	25,000	Sep	2511 Revere Avenue	Dayton	OH	45420	937-258-1104	B
OH	Oktoberfest	32,000	Oct	456 Belmont Park N.	Dayton	OH	45405	513-223-5277	B
OH	Groveport Festival Of The Arts	5,000	Sep	655 Blacklick St	Groveport	OH	43125	614-836-5301	B
OH	Kent Art In The Park	21,000	Sep	497 Middlebury Road	Kent	OH	44240	330-673-8897	B
OH	Lakewood Arts Festival	15,000	Aug	P O Box 771288	Lakewood	OH	44107	216-521-7063	B
OH	Butler Prairie Peddler Old West Fest.	32,000	Oct	P. O. Box 287	Norwalk	OH	44857	419-663-1818	B

OH	Sauerkraut Fest	300,000	Oct	P. O. Box 281	Waynes-ville	OH	45068	513-897-8855	B
OK	Tulsa International Mayfest	300,000	May	201 W. 5th Ste. 460	Tulsa	OK	74103	918-582-6435	A
OK	An Affair Of The Heart		Oct	P. O. Box 890778	Oklahoma City	OK	73189	405-632-2652	A-
OK	Spring Festival Of The Arts	700,000	Apr	400 W. Califor-nia	Oklahoma City	OK	73102	405-270-4848	A+
OK	Downtown Edmond Art Festival	50,000	Apr	P. O. Box 3653	Edmond	OK	73083	405-249-9391	B
OK	Arts For All Festival	23,000	May	P. O. Box 592	Lawton	OK	73502	580-248-5384	B
OK	Paseo Arts Festival	40,000	May	3000 North Lee	Oklahoma City	OK	73103	405-525-2688	B
OR	Artquake-Art Street	200,000	Aug	P O Box 9100	Portland	OR	97207	503-227-2787	A
OR	Fall Festival	25,000	Sep	420 Nw Second	Corvalis	OR	97330	503-757-1505	A-
OR	Oregon Country Fair	50,000	Jul	P. O. Box 2972	Eugene	OR	97402	541-343-4298	A-
OR	Salem Art Fair & Festival	110,000	Jul	600 Mission St.	Salem	OR	97302	503-581-2228	A-
OR	Wah Change Northwest Art And Air	30,000	Aug	P. O. Box 490	Albany	OR	97321	541-917-7777	B
OR	Lake Oswego Festival Of The Arts	25,000	Jun	P. O. Box 385	Lake Oswego	OR	97034	503-636-1060	B
PA	German-town Friends Craft Show	5,000	Mar	31 W Coulter St	Philadel-phia	PA	19144	215-951-2340	A
PA	Manayunk Arts Festival	250,000	Jun	111 Grape Street	Philadel-phia	PA	19127	215-482-9565	A

PA	Three Rivers Art Festival	600,000	Jun	707 Penn Ave.	Pittsburgh	PA	15222	412-281-8723	A
PA	Central Penn.Festival Of The Arts	150,000	Jul	P O Box 1023	State College	PA	16804	814-237-3682	A
PA	Penn's Colony Festival	50,000	Sep	P. O. Box 247	Allison Park	PA	15101	724-352-9922	A-
PA	National Apple Harvest Festival	100,000	Oct	P. O. Box 38	Biglerville	PA	17307	717-677-9413	A-
PA	Arts And Crafts Colonial Festival	40,000	Sep	P. O. Box 166	Irwin	PA	15642	724-863-4577	A-
PA	Kutztown Festival	110,000	Jun	P. O. Box 306	Kutztown	PA	19530	610-285-0368	A-
PA	Long's Park Art And Craft Fes	17,000	Aug	P. O. Box 1553	Lancaster	PA	17608	717-295-7054	A-
PA	Westmoreland Arts And Heritage Fest.	250,000	Jul	Rr2, Box 355a	Latrobe	PA	15650	724-834-7474	A-
PA	Fort Ligonier Days	100,000	Oct	120 East Main	Ligonier	PA	15658	724-238-4200	A-
PA	Mt Gretna Outdoor Art Sh.	20,000	Aug	P. O. Box 561	Mt Gretna	PA	17064	717-964-2340	A-
PA	A Fair In The Park (Mellon Park)	25,000	Sep	340 Bigbee St, #2	Pittsburgh	PA	15211	412-431-6270	A-
PA	Greater Pittsburgh Holiday Sp.	19,000	Nov	P. O. Box 166	Irwin	PA	15642	724-863-4577	A-
PA	Buyers Markets Of American Craft	10,000	Feb	3000 Chestnut Avenue, #300	Baltimore	MD	21211	410-889-2933	A+
PA	Dutch Folk Festival	50,000	Jun	3760 Layfield Road	Penns-burg	PA	18073	215-679-9610	A+

PA	Philadel-phia Mus. Of Art Craft Show	30,000	Nov	P. O. Box 7646	Philadel-phia	PA	19101	215-684-7931	A+
PA	Shadyside Summer Arts Festival	150,000	Aug	P. O. Box 4866	Pittsburgh	PA	15206	412-621-8481	A+
PA	Mayfair Festival Of The Arts	400,000	May	2020 Hamilton St	Allentown	PA	18104	610-437-6900	B
PA	Fall Pumpkin Fest	24,000	Oct	P. O. Box 646	Conneaut Lake	PA	16316	800-332-2338	B
PA	Celebrate Erie	75,000	Aug	626 Sate Street Room 500	Erie	PA	16501	814-870-1269	B
PA	Ford City Area Heritage Days	100,000	Jul	P. O. Box 205	Ford City	PA	16226	724-783-1617	B
PA	Pymatuning Pioneer And Art Festival	20,000	Jul	P. O. Box 146	James-town	PA	16134	724-927-9473	B
PA	Heart Of Lancaster County A And C	20,000	Sep	P. O. Box 257	Lititz	PA	17543	717-626-7369	B
PA	New Hope Arts And Crafts Festival	20,000	Oct	P. O. Box 633	New Hope	PA	18938	215-598-3301	B
PA	Annual State Craft Fair	18,000	Jul	10 Stable Mill Trail	Richboro	PA	18954	215-579-5997	B
PA	Tall Oaks Autumn Fest In Woods	50,000	Sep	154 Star Route	Sheffield	PA	16347	814-968-5558	B
PA	Mountain Craft Days	14,000	Sep	10649 Somerset Pike	Somerset	PA	15501	814-445-6077	B
PA	Yorkfest	20,000	Aug	1 West Market Street	York	PA	17401	717-848-9339	B
RI	Wickford Fine Art Festival	60,000	Jul	36 Beach St.	Wickford	RI	02852	401-295-4075	A-

RI	Scituate Art Festival	100,000	Oct	P. O. Box 126	North Scituate	RI	02857	401-647-0057	A+
RI	Virtu Art Festival	20,000	May	1 Chamber Way	Westerly	RI	02891	401-596-7761	B
SC	Flowertown Festival	250,000	Mar	140 South Cedar Street	Summer-ville	SC	29483	843-871-9622	A
SC	Aiken's Makin's	30,000	Sep	P. O. Box 892	Aiken	SC	29801	803-641-1111	B
SC	Columbia Fine Art And Craft Show	25,000	Sep	P. O. Box 347	Ardmore	PA	19003	877-244-9768	B
SC	Craft Show At Piccolo Spoleto	10,000	May	P. O. Box 22152	Charles-ton	SC	29413	843-723-2938	B
SC	Southeast-ern Arts & Crafts Expo	70,000	Sep	1112 Bull St	Columbia	SC	29201	803-343-2155	B
SC	Atalaya Arts & Crafts Festival	10,000	Sep	1205 Pendleto n St	Columbia	SC	29201	803-734-0517	B
SC	Craftsmens Classic	30,000	Oct	1240 Oakland Ave	Greens-boro	NC	27403	336-274-5550	B
SC	Craftsmens Classic A and C	20,000	Aug	1240 Oakland Ave	Greens-boro	NC	27403	336-274-5550	B
SC	Coastal Carolina Fair, Ladson	250,000	Oct	P. O. Box 762	Ladson	SC	29456	843-572-3161	B
SC	Myrtle Beach Arts And Fall Festival	90,000	Oct	1325 Celebrity Circle	Myrtle Beach	SC	29577	706-840-1877	B
SC	Ware Shoals Catfish Festival	25,000	May	P. O. Box 510	Ware Shoals	SC	29692	864-456-7664	B
SD	Summer Arts Festival	50,000	Jul	P O Box 555	Brookings	SD	57006	605-693-4595	A
SD	Aberdeen Arts In The Park	20,000	Jun	P. O. Box 126	Aberdeen	SD	57402	605-226-1557	B

SD	Sioux Falls Sidewalk Arts Festival	50,000	Sep	301 South Main Street	Sioux Falls	SD	57104	605-367-7397	B
TN	Taca Fall Crafts	40,000	Sep	P O Box 120066	Nashville	TN	37212	615-385-1904	A
TN	Art In The Park	45,000	Oct	3100 Walnut Grove # 402	Memphis	TN	38111	901-761-1278	A-
TN	Harvest Crafts Festival	35,000	Oct	2354 Chap-man Hwy	Sevierville	TN	37876	423-453-3497	A-
TN	Ketner's Mill Country Fair	25,000	Oct	P. O. Box 1447	Chatta-nooga	TN	37401	615-821-3238	A+
TN	Pink Palace Crafts Fair	40,000	Oct	3050 Central Ave.	Memphis	TN	38111	901-320-6408	A+
TN	American Artisan Festival	50,000	Jun	4231 Harding	Nashville	TN	37205	615-298-4691	A+
TN	Memphis Fine Art Show	25,000	Jun	P. O. Box 347	Ardmore	PA	19003	877-244-9768	B
TN	Webb School Arts And Crafts	85,000	Oct	P. O. Box 222	Bell Buckle	TN	37020	931-389-6784	B
TN	Meriwether Lewis Arts And Crafts	30,000	Oct	P. O. Box 676	Columbia	TN	38401	931-381-9494	B
TN	Holiday Market A And C Memphis	12,000	Nov	P. O. Box 1327	Cordova	TN	38088	901-854-6589	B
TN	Unicoi County Apple Fest.	90,000	Oct	P. O. Box 713	Erwin	TN	37650	423-743-3000	B
TN	Lenoir City Arts And Crafts Fest.	15,000	Jun	P. O. Box 183	Lenoir City	TN	37771	865-986-7757	B
TN	Christmas Village	30,000	Nov	P O Box 158826	Nashville	TN	37215	615-320-5353	B
TX	Laguna Gloria Festival	30,000	May	P. O. Box 5705	Austin	TX	78763	512-458-6073	A

TX	Artfest / The 500, Inc.	80,000	May	11300 N Central, #415	Dallas	TX	75243	214-565-0200	A
TX	Cottonwood Arts Festival	20,000	Oct	711 West Arapaho	Richardson	TX	75080	214-231-4624	A
TX	Spring Fling	20,000	Apr	2 Eureka Circle	Wichita Falls	TX	76308	940-692-0923	A-
TX	Armadillo Christmas Bazaar	35,000	Dec	4428 Gillis St.	Austin	TX	78745	512-447-1605	A+
TX	Main Street Fort Worth Arts Festival	40,000	Apr	306 W 7th St, #400	Fort Worth	TX	76102	817-336-ARTS	A+
TX	Shrimpo Ree Of Texas	55,000	Jun	P. O. Box 1949	Aransas Pass	TX	78335	361-758-2750	B
TX	The Peddler Show/Arlington	20,000	Nov	5508 Hwy 290 West #208	Austin	TX	78735	512-358-1000	B
TX	Bryan College Station Arts And Music	25,000	Sep	3160 Bee Caves Road #201	Austin	TX	78704	512-441-9015	B
TX	The Peddler Show/Fredericksburg	20,000	Nov	5508 Hwy 290 West #208	Austin	TX	78735	512-358-1000	B
TX	Scarecrow Festival	20,000	Oct	9220 Poplar Street	Chappel Hill	TX	77426	979-836-6033	B
TX	Fulton Oysterfest	30,000	Mar	P. O. Box 393	Fulton	TX	78358	361-729-2388	B
TX	Dickens On The Strand	42,000	Nov	502 20th Street	Galveston	TX	77550	409-765-7834	B
TX	Georgetown Red Poppy Festival	25,000	Apr	P.O. Box 409	Georgetown	TX	78627	512-930-3545	B
TX	Granbury Arts And Crafts Festival	45,000	Jul	3408 East Highway 377	Granbury	TX	76049	817-573-1622	B

TX	Conroe Cajun Catfish Fest.	35,000	Oct	P. O. Box 541992	Houston	TX	77254	713-863-9994	B
TX	The Houston International Fest.	500,000	Apr	1221 Lamar, #715	Houston	TX	77010	714-654-8808	B
TX	Keller Festival	20,000	May	P. O. Box 761	Keller	TX	76244	817-498-1292	B
TX	Texas State Arts And Crafts Fair	20,000	May	P. O. Box 1527	Kerrville	TX	78029	210-896-5711	B
TX	Lubbock Arts Festival	30,000	Apr	2109 Broadway	Lubbock	TX	79401	806-744-2787	B
TX	Poteet Strawberry Festival	75,000	Apr	P. O. Box 227	Poteet	TX	78065	830-276-8436	B
TX	Christmas At Old Fort Concho	20,000	Dec	630 South Oakes	San Angelo	TX	76903	325-657-4441	B
TX	San Antonio Memorial Day A And C	45,000	May	110 Broadway, Ste 60	San Antonio	TX	78205	210-227-4286	B
TX	Fiesta Arts Fair	20,000	Apr	300 Augusta	San Antonio	TX	78205	210-224-1848	B
TX	Art On The Square		Apr	P. O. Box 92611	Southlake	TX	76092	817-421-6792	B
TX	Texarkana Quadrangle Art And Music	35,000	Sep	P. O. Box 2343	Texarkana	TX	75504	903-793-4831	B
TX	Parker County Peach Fest	35,000	Jul	P. O. Box 310	Weatherford	TX	76086	888-594-3801	B
UT	The Utah Arts Festival	69,000	Jun	331 W. Pierpolnt Ave	Salt Lake City	UT	84101	801-322-2428	A
UT	Park City Art Festival	70,000	Aug	P O Box 1478	Park City	UT	84060	801-649-8882	A+
UT	Salt Lake Family	25,000	Nov	P. O. Box 2815	Kirkland	WA	98083	800-521-7469	B

UT	America's Freedom Fest. Provo	100,000	Jul	P. O. Box F	Provo	UT	84603	801-431-0027	B
UT	St George Art Festival	15,000	Apr	86 S Main St.	St George	UT	84770	801-634-5850	B
VA	Crozet Arts & Crafts Festival	10,000	May	P O Box 699	Crozet	VA	22932	804-977-0406	A
VA	Craftsmens Classic Arts And Crafts	20,000	Oct	1240 Oakland Ave	Greens-boro	NC	27403	336-274-5550	A
VA	Occoquan Fall Arts And Crafts	200,000	Sep	P. O. Box 258	Occoquan	VA	22125	703-491-2168	A
VA	Christmas Market	23,000	Nov	P. O. Box 909	Virginia Beach	VA	23451	757-417-7771	A
VA	Virginia Craft And Folk Art Fest	6,000	Oct	P. O. Box 310	Cashtown	PA	17310	717-337-3060	A-
VA	Ghent Art Show	45,000	May	2308 Granby St	Norfolk,	VA	23517	804-446-2250	A-
VA	Hand Workshop Craft & Dsn. Show	10,000	Nov	1812 West Main St.	Richmond	VA	23220	804-353-009	A-
VA	Festival In The Park-Craft Show	375,000	May	P. O. Box 8276	Roanoke	VA	24014	703-342-2640	A-
VA	Neptune Fest Art And Craft Show	250,000	Sep	2200 Parks Ave	Virginia Beach	VA	23451	757-425-0000	A-
VA	An Occas-ion For The Arts	15,000	Oct	P O Box 1520	Williams-burg	VA	23187	804-229-5450	A-
VA	Craftsmens Christmas Classic	35,000	Nov	P. O. Box 305	Chase City	VA	23924	434-372-3996	A+
VA	Virginia Carolina Craftsmen	30,000	Nov	1240 Oakland Ave	Greens-boro	NC	27403	910-274-5550	A+
VA	Northern Va Fine Arts Festival	50,000	May	11911 Freedom Drive Ste 110	Reston	VA	20190	703-471-9242	A+

VA	Richmond Fine Art & Craft Show	25,000	Aug	P. O. Box 347	Ardmore	PA	19003	877-244-9768	B
VA	City Of Fairfax Fall Festival	40,000	Oct	3730 Old Lee Highway	Fairfax	VA	22030	703-385-7949	B
VA	Taste Of The Mountains	20,000	Sep	P. O. Box 373	Madison	VA	22727	540-948-4455	B
VA	Manassas Fall Jubilee	20,000	Oct	9431 West Street	Manassas	VA	20110	703-361-6599	B
VA	Gosport Arts Festival	60,000	May	1211 Colley Avenue #1	Norfolk	VA	23517	757-446-2250	B
VA	Stockley Gardens Spring Arts Fest	25,000	May	801 Boush St. Ste 302	Norfolk,	VA	23510	757-625-6161	B
VA	Boardwalk Art Show	300,000	Jun	2200 Parks Ave	Virginia Beach	VA	23451	757-425-0000	B
VA	Waterford Fair	30,000	Oct	P. O. Box 142	Waterford	VA	20197	540-882-3018	B
VA	Richmond Holiday Arts And Crafts	15,000	Oct	P. O. Box 11565	Winston-Salem	NC	27116	336-924-4539	B
VT	Art In The Park	7,000	Aug	16 S. Main St.	Rutland	VT	05701	802-775-0356	A-
VT	Hildene Folage Art And Craft	14,000	Oct	P. O. Box 538	Putney	VT	05346	802-387-5772	B
WA	Northwest Folklife Festival	220,000	May	305 Harrison Street	Seattle	WA	98109	206-684-7327	A
WA	Art Museum Fair	280,000	Jul	510 Bellevue Way NE	Bellevue	WA	98004	425-519-0742	A-
WA	Sixth Street Fair & Taste Of Bellevue	50,000	Jul	500 108th Ave, NE Ste 210	Bellevue	WA	98004	206-453-1223	A-

WA	Allied Artists Sidewalk Show	45,000	Jul	89 Lee Boulevard	Richland	WA	99362	509-375-1345	A-
WA	Festival Of The Arts	250,000	Jul	1916 Pike Place, #146	Seattle	WA	98101	206-363-2048	A+
WA	Anacortes Arts & Crafts Festival	50,000	Aug	819 Commer-ial, Suite E.	Anacortes	WA	98221	360-293-6211	B
WA	Battle Ground Harvest Days	35,000	Jul	912 East Main Street	Battle Ground	WA	98604	360-687-1510	B
WA	Camas Days	20,000	Jul	P. O. Box 919	Camas	WA	98607	206-834-2472	B
WA	Coupeville Arts And Crafts Festival	20,000	Aug	P. O. Box 611	Coupeville	WA	98239	360-678-5116	B
WA	Tidefest	5,000	Dec	5101 Rosedale St, Nw	Gig Harbor	WA	98335	206-851-6131	B
WA	Issaquah Salmon Days Festival	150,000	Oct	155 Nw Gilman Blvd	Issaquah	WA	98027	206-270-2532	B
WA	Summer-fest: Art And Wine Waterfront	35,000	Jul	620 Market Street	Kirkland	WA	98033	425-822-7161	B
WA	Tacoma Holiday Food And Gift Fest.	45,000	Oct	P. O. Box 2815	Kirkland	WA	98083	800-521-7469	B
WA	Skagit Valley Tulip Festival Fair	20,000	Apr	P O Box 1801	Mount Vernon	WA	98273	360-336-9277	B
WA	Celebrate Lavender Festival	30,000	Jul	105 1/2 East First St.	Port Angeles	WA	98362	877-681-3035	B
WA	North Kitsap Arts And Crafts Fest.	30,000	Jul	P. O. Box 2043	Poulsbo	WA	98370	360-297-2490	B

WA	A Victorian Country Christmas	45,000	Nov	P. O. Box 73129	Puyallup	WA	98373	253-770-0777	B
WA	Christmas Memories	17,000	Nov	619 Meadows Drive East	Richland	WA	99352	509-627-1854	B
WA	University District Street Fair	200,000	May	4714 University Way N E, #516	Seattle	WA	98105	206-523-4272	B
WA	Spokane Christmas Arts And Crafts	15,000	Nov	P. O. Box 14987	Spokane	WA	99214	509-924-0588	B
WI	Oconomo-woc Fest Of The Arts	25,000	Aug	P O Box 651	Oconomo-woc	WI	53066	414-567-1243	A
WI	Wausau Festival Of The Arts	30,000	Sep	P O Box 1763	Wausau	WI	54402	715-842-1676	A
WI	Craft Fair Usa	18,000	Oct	9312 West National Ave	West Allis	WI	53227	414-321-2100	A
WI	Mt. Mary Starving Artist Fair	15,000	Sep	17160 Deer Park Dr.	Brookfield	WI	53005	(NO) PHONE	A+
WI	Art Fair On The Square	200,000	Jul	211 State St	Madison	WI	53703	608-257-0158	A+
WI	Lakefront Festival Of Arts	50,000	Jun	750 N. Art Mus-um Dr	Milwaukee	WI	53202	414-224-3200	A+
WI	Art In The Park	25,000	Aug	130 N Morrison St	Appleton	WI	54911	414-733-4089	B
WI	Madison Autumn A And C Affair	15,000	Dec	P. O. Box 184	Boys Town	NE	68010	402-331-2889	B
WI	Ozaukee Center Harvest Festival	30,000	Sep	W62 N718 River--edge Dr.	Cedarburg	WI	53012	262-377-8230	B
WI	Artstreet	600,000	Aug	P O Box 704	Green Bay	WI	54305	414-435-2787	B

WI	Holy Hill Arts And Crafts Fair	15,000	Sep	1525 Carmel Road	Hubertus	WI	53033	262-966-7172	B
WI	The Mile Of Art	5,000	Aug	6801 N Yates Rd.	Milwaukee	WI	53217	414-351-7516	B
WI	Morning Glory Crafts Fair	10,000	Aug	1630 E Royall Pl.	Milwaukee	WI	53202	414-278-8295	B
WI	Mount Horeb Art Fair	15,000	Jul	P. O. Box 84	Mount Horeb	WI	53572	608-437-5914	B
WI	Outdoor Arts Fest	25,000	Jul	608 New York Ave	Sheboy-gan	WI	53081	920-458-6144	B
WI	Townline Art Fair	5,000	Oct	10376 Hwy 42	Sister Bay	WI	54234	414-854-4343	B
WI	Watermelon Days Craft Fest	15,000	Jul	705 Bugbee Avenue	Wausau	WI	54401	715-675-6201	B
WI	Apple Harvest Craft Fair	13,000	Sep	705 Bugbee Avenue	Wausau	WI	54401	715-675-6201	B
WI	Art World	30,000	Sep	705 Bugbee Avenue	Wausau	WI	54401	715-675-6201	B
WV	Mountain State Arts & Craft Fair	30,000	Jul	P. O. Box 389	Ripley	WV	25271	304-372-8159	A
WV	Mountain Heritage Art & Craft Fest.	25,000	Sep	P O Box 426	Charles Town	WV	25414	800-624-0577	A+
WV	W. Virginia Strawberry Festival	65,000	May	P. O. Box 117	Buchan-non	WV	26201	304-473-8122	B
WV	New River Gorge Bridge Day	70,000	Oct	310 Oyler Avenue	Oak Hill	WV	25901	304-658-5574	B
WV	Firemen's Craft Fest	25,000	Sep	R.R. 3, Box 35	Phillippi	WV	26416		B
WV	Oglebayfest Artists' Market	50,000	Oct	1330 National Rd.	Wheeling	WV	26003	304-242-7700	B
WY	Mtn. Artists Rendez-vous	7,000	Jul	P. O. Box 1248	Jackson Hole	WY	83001	307-733-8792	B

Conclusion

As a skilled craftsperson, you will always have a source of income, because the public will always appreciate the beautiful things that you make. You have only to educate the customer as to why your locally handmade products are worth more money than their global counterparts (cheap imports.) The heart-felt appreciation by the customer for the craftsperson who is committed to quality and uniqueness makes the sacrifices and uncertainties of this unique lifestyle worthwhile.

In writing this book, I hope I have given you some new insights into how to improve your craft business, and shown you how a computer can assist you. I know you will find a use for many of the tips, addresses, and spreadsheets. The ones you don't use today may be helpful to you in the coming years as you modify your approach to marketing your craft products.

This book is updated with every new printing, so if you have any comments, corrections, sources, ideas for new forms, or criticisms, please take a moment to email me at eagleab@aol.com

More Books from Craftmasters

Microsoft Office for Artists and Craftspeople 128 pages, CD-Rom, $39.95
This book and CD has, in addition to the forms in this "Make Money" book, another 50 spreadsheets for managing your craft business, including forms for an employee application, non-competing agreement, credit application, budget, starting your own gallery, project bid, letter templates for bad checks and other business letters, and more.

How to Put On a Great Craft Show 68 Pages, $29.95
Have you ever thought about putting on your craft show? This book will help you make your first show and every show a lucrative event! All the information you need to organize an exciting craft fair or art show is here! Written by Lee Spiegel, former director of the Crafts Fair Guide.

CD-Rom with spreadsheets, craft galleries, fonts, and clip art $19.95
This is a CD with all the spreadsheets in this book, a Microsoft excel file with the 1100 craft galleries so you can print mailing labels, and a bonus of 200 fonts and 10,000 b/w clip art images for logos and other design ideas.

To order any of the above publications, go to www.craftmasters.com

precisely

Notes

Made in the USA
Lexington, KY
21 November 2010